THE COMPLETE GUIDE TO
POLO

THE COMPLETE GUIDE TO

POLO

Lauren Dibble

J. A. ALLEN · LONDON

First published in 2015 by
J. A. Allen
Clerkenwell House
Clerkenwell Green
London ECIR OHT

J. A. Allen is an imprint of Robert Hale Limited
www.allenbooks.co.uk

ISBN 978-1-908809-34-6

British Library Cataloguing in Publication Data
A catalogue record for this book is available from the British Library

Design and typesetting by Paul Saunders
Edited by Martin Diggle

Photographs on pages by 2, 32, 34, 39, 42, 43, 45, 50, 51, 58 (top), 60, 62, 70, 76, 80, 88,
92, 98, 100, 102, 106 and 136 Jessica Patterson
Photography; on pages 12, 24, 29, 33, 38, 56, 58 (bottom), 59, 90, 105 and 136 by
Shutterstock.com; other photographs by the author
Line drawings by Carole Vincer

Printed in Singapore by Craft Print International Ltd

This book is dedicated to all the people who have supported me in my polo journey: the teachers, the students, the players and the fans. To all of the polo ponies who have given their heart and soul to pack me around the field. To my loving and understanding husband, for supporting me in my passion, and to my mother, without whose support I would never have been introduced to the sport I love so much.

Contents

Foreword

I STARTED A BIT LATE but played polo for about 25 years from 1971 as an amateur and managed to scrabble up to 4 goals – but things were a bit different in those days. I left the army in 1999 and have been very fortunate to have been Chief Executive of the Hurlingham Polo Association since then, paid to do a job I really enjoy.

I hope that this book will give everyone, from the novice player to the more experienced, a solid foundation in their polo education, including some of the traditions and legends of our great sport.

As a player, this book gives you a primer on the how and the why behind the equipment we choose to use and Lauren provides the reader with tips and tricks for how to improve the relationship with your pony; we're all familiar with the saying that your mount is 80 per cent of the game.

Chapter 4, The Swing, focuses on the biomechanics of the swing and how to perfect your accuracy with the ball before Lauren provides an over-all picture of the field, how to play different positions effectively and make the most out of your team. The final chapter is an excellent summary of the HPA and the USPA rule books.

Lauren believes that knowledge is the key to better polo and she has written this book as if she were your personal trainer, standing by your side on the polo field. There is something here for everyone, so here's to better polo!

David Woodd
Chief Executive of Hurlingham Polo Association

Introduction

I WAS FIRST INTRODUCED to polo by a friend of a friend. I believe most of us have similar stories. I had ridden working hunters (USA *hunter/ jumpers*) since I was a child, but grew bored with it around my teenage years and hung up my jodhpurs. A few years later, a friend of the family, who had played for a very long time, encouraged my mother to take me out to my first lesson. After a brief introduction, and a good bit of time frustratingly trying to whack this tiny ball with a long mallet, we played a very slow-paced chukka (USA *chukker*). Our trainer would stop us, point out things we'd done right, things we'd done wrong, and encourage us to start again. Halfway through I found myself practically hanging off the stirrups, hand on my pony's neck, reaching to hook an 'opponent' and froze. What in the world was I doing? I'd never done anything so foolish. But I had to admit, I was hooked.

Those slow, painful lessons, on those oh-so-patient ponies, with my instructor correcting us with his thick Chilean accent became the highlight of my summer weeks. I eventually went on to work for this same instructor, learned from him how to train polo ponies, lived in the barns along with the grooms, and eventually began teaching lessons for this same instructor. He cultivated an absolute addiction within me: I couldn't get enough. I played as much as I could, worked as much as I could, and absorbed as much knowledge as I possibly could.

One thing I did find frustrating in my quest for more information was the lack of formal education, or knowledge out there. Most of the books I've found on the subject (and I have amassed a small library) tend to be very basic; things that anyone who has played for more than a season probably already knows. On top of that, it seems that most of work written on the subject is from the 1920s and 30s.

One reason for the preponderance of books from that time is that polo achieved perhaps its greatest era of popularity in the 1920s. Thousands of spectators would regularly attend public games, play-by-play action was broadcast over the radio to the general public, and many well-known actors and politicians played. For a while, the sport declined

It is easy to become hooked on the thrills of polo.

in popularly as a result of the socio-economic pressures of the Second World War, but in more recent times it is showing a steady resurgence. Today, there are more polo clubs and more players than the world has seen in a while. Whether we're back to our pre-war numbers, I cannot tell, but there is a huge movement of resurrection taking place.

The average player nowadays has a similar story to mine. They get introduced to the sport through a friend of a friend, become irrevocably hooked, and want to learn more in order to be the best that they possibly can be. But where do they turn? Often, their instructors and fellow players do not have the answers to their questions. Why do they use a Pelham for that particular pony? Why do ponies sport polo wraps? When it is appropriate to hit a back shot as opposed to turning the ball? How are you *supposed* to hit the ball? How can you get better?

This book is my attempt at covering absolutely everything I have learned. Through my degree in Equine Studies, I bring a scientific but traditional approach to horsemanship, horse husbandry, nutrition and confirmation. Through my 15+ years of playing, riding, working, training and teaching polo, I bring first-hand experience and know-how, developed from years through a process of elimination. Through my travels around the world, I bring a knowledge of how others play the sport, and different techniques used to accomplish the same goal. Through a diligent study of all available published material on the subject, I bring a thorough foundation and understanding of how the sport has been played, and how it should be played in the future. My hope is that all of these different avenues have helped me to compile a complete guide to polo; one that will encompass everything an enthusiastic player wants and will need to know.

When you know more as a polo player, you will be more effective, and better equipped to be the best player you can be, and to play the best polo you can. Here's to playing great polo!

CHAPTER ONE

The History of Polo

MAN'S FIRST INTERACTION with horses almost certainly took the form of hunting them as a food source, but the increase in equine fossils found in archaeological sites in countries such as Kazakhstan and Ukraine leads us to believe that, roughly 6,000 years ago, horses were domesticated – initially for the same purpose – along similar lines to cattle. Other sites have excavated tack, and the dates of these excavations suggest that, by around 3,500 BC (i.e. around 5,500 years ago), man had advanced to using horses for draught and pack purposes, and then to riding them.

Once the possibilities of driving and riding had been recognised, one of the key uses of horses was in warfare, drawing chariots or being ridden by cavalry. Certainly, by 3,000 BC the mounted soldier had become a force to be reckoned with. A man on horseback could travel much further and faster than one on foot and could conserve his energy for battle. The cavalry was more manoeuvrable than infantry, had a height/weight advantage, and was a highly valuable part of any army.

As the practice of riding developed, so did the idea of using this skill in sporting contexts. Mounted hunting and forms of racing were probably the first of these but, as time went on, more and more equestrian sports came into being.

THE BEGINNINGS OF POLO

While the exact date of the first polo match is unknown, in ancient Persia around 600 BC there was a game called *chaugán*, which refers to the polo mallet. It was played with hundreds of players to a side and was designed to mimic war, giving soldiers ample practice. Just like archery, swordplay and falconry, this early form of polo became an excellent pastime for teaching young warriors and nobility the skills needed for battle. As armies throughout Asia began using the horse in battle, this form of polo became a major aspect of training.

An anecdotal tale of Alexander the Great tells of the Persian King Darius III (370–330 BC), who refused to pay Alexander a bribe for safety. When Alexander threatened to attack, Darius sent him a *chaugán* stick and ball, a tongue-in-cheek reference to Alexander's immaturity and inexperience in war and diplomacy. Alexander's reply was, 'The ball is the Earth and I am the stick.'

Manipur, a state in India, became the ancient headquarters for polo. It was considered one of three forms of hockey the country played (field hockey, wrestling hockey, and polo) and was known as *kan-jai-bazéé*. (Under this name, or *sagol kangjei*, the sport was also popular in the Himalayan region around the fifteenth century.) Although the oldest polo grounds in Manipur dated to around AD 33, local rituals to 'Marjing', a winged-pony god of polo, and his son, 'Khori-Phaba', the polo-playing god of sports, indicate that polo has a much older origin in India.

In Manipur, polo was not just a pastime for the nobility or cavalry. The Royal Polo grounds, within the ramparts of the Kangla Fort, is called Manung Kangjei Bung, or 'Inner Polo Grounds'. Public games were, and still are, held at the Mapan Kangjei Bung, or 'Outer Polo Grounds'.

Although the Chinese were the next to pick up the sport, Japan followed close after. The first recorded polo match in Japan was said to have taken place in AD 727.

Meanwhile, in Iran, polo became the national sport, enjoyed by women as well as men. In the sixth century AD, it was recorded that the

Queen of Iran was brazen enough to challenge the King at the time, King Khosrow II Parviz, to a match.

In the ninth century, the Iranian historian Dinvari wrote of polo: 'Polo requires a great deal of exercise … If a polo stick breaks during a game it is a sign of inefficiency … A player should strictly avoid using strong language and should be patient and temperate.'

In the eleventh century, Omar Khayyám, a Persian poet, used polo as a metaphor for the human condition and Mankind's relationship to God:

> *The Ball no Question makes of Ayes and Noes,*
> *But Right or Left as strikes the Player goes,*
> *And He that toss'd Thee down into the Field,*
> *He knows about it all—HE knows—HE knows!*

In the thirteenth century, the poet Nizami Ganjavi wrote an epic love story based around the polo matches between King Khosrow II Parviz and his courtiers and the beautiful Princess Shirin and her ladies-in-waiting, mentioned above. In this story, King Khosrow kills his rival, Farhad, for the affections of Shirin. Khosrow then embarks on long journeys, physically and spiritually, before returning to his love, marrying her, and producing a son with her. His son eventually murders him, and his wife ends up committing suicide over the body of her dead husband. This epic love story influenced many Persian writers who followed Nizami Ganjavi.

Polo in the Middle Ages was a very different sport from the one we know now. The game consisted of two 30-minute chukkas, riders used only one mount, and the game was stopped only for serious injury. If the ball went out of bounds, it was immediately thrown back in by a spectator. Fouls did not exist and every man played for himself. This style of play, combined with the stone goal-posts, meant that serious injury and death were commonplace on the polo field. In 1210, Sultan Qutb-ud-din Aibak, the Turkish Emperor of Northern India, died during a polo match when his mount flipped over backwards and he was impaled on the pommel of his saddle.

POLO IN THE NINETEENTH CENTURY

Unfortunately, not much was written about polo between the fifteenth and nineteenth centuries, although it is known that a polo field was built in the Persian city of Ispahan by Shah Abbas the Great (ruled 1585–1628), and that the sixteenth-century Indian ruler Akbar the Great had polo fields in Agra, which are still in place. We also know that, as the sport grew and spread, the word that we use for it now became increasingly the recognised term, being derived from the Tibetan *pulu* (ball).

In 1859, English Army Lieutenant Joseph Sherer played his first 'pulu' game in Manipur. Smitten by the game, he established the first European Polo Club in India later that same year. This fast, exciting sport spread quickly throughout the British military stations as an excellent distraction from military life, and an effective means of teaching young cavalry officers prowess in the saddle.

The sport of polo was then brought to England by someone who had never even seen a game. In 1869, Captain Edward 'Chicken' Hartopp (1845–82) read an article in *The Field* magazine, about the game that the British cavalry were playing in Manipur and said it sounded 'a good game that they have in India'. Hartopp recruited several other soldiers and, riding cavalry chargers, they used a cricket ball and walking sticks and/or golf clubs as mallets. Since they had only a rudimentary understanding of the rules, one can only imagine how frustrating that match must have been. Nonetheless it was enjoyable enough, and they continued to play. It soon became apparent that cavalry chargers were not the most suitable polo mounts, so Captain William Chaine was sent to Ireland to find better ponies. He returned with seventeen.

Shortly thereafter, the 10th Hussars returned to Hounslow from their summer drills, and challenged the 9th Lancers to a polo match. The Lancers accepted the challenge, and the first official polo match in

England was played on 28 June 1870. This match attracted royal attention. HRH the Prince of Wales and Princess Alexandra, along with Prince Arthur and the Duke of Cambridge, Queen Victoria's cousin and the Commander-in-Chief of the British Army, all attended, eager to witness this sport brought back from India.

One of the players of this game, Lieutenant-Colonel Thomas St Quintin, later commented that game-play resembled more of a rugby scrimmage, with everyone bumping and pushing into one another in a crowd, with no idea of where the ball was. Regardless, everyone seemed to enjoy themselves, and the game was officially a hit.

Shortly after this, the first official polo club in Britain was founded by Captain Francis 'Tip' Herbert at Monmouthshire near Abergavenny, in Wales. By 1874, polo had reached The Hurlingham Club in West London. Founded as a shooting club, Hurlingham had the space to mark out two polo fields, and quickly adopted the sport. The first game to be played there was between the 1st Life Guards and the Royal Horse Guards on 6 June 1874, again with royalty in attendance. The following year the first set of English rules were drawn up by the then Hurlingham Polo Committee. It was a still unruly game, with eight or more players a side, and matches lasting all afternoon.

The game was usually played in military saddles, with long stirrup leathers and a deep seat. Play began with two opposing players on the fastest ponies who charged to the centre of the field from behind their respective goal-lines, fought for possession of the ball, and tried to score without assistance. (The rest of the team was on the field for the duration of the game, but there was no passing. If one team member lost possession of the ball, another would swoop in to take possession.) The game was by now played on a much smaller field than previously: 300 x 600 feet, and the offside fore shot (see page 91) was the only one used.

Via Captain Hartopp, the game spread to Ireland in 1872, to the USA and Argentina in 1875 and to Canada in 1883. David Shennan, a British settler, actually organised the first game in Argentina on 3 September 1875. The game was an instant hit and thrived because of the existing equestrian culture of the Argentine gauchos. The River Plate Polo

Association was founded in 1892 and would eventually be the foundation for the current Asociación Argentina de Polo.

In 1876, Lieutenant-Colonel Thomas St Quintin brought the game with him to Australia. While he was officially known as the 'Father of Australian Polo', it was his brothers who stayed on and helped the sport progress.

In 1876, *New York Herald* owner, James Gordon Bennett Jr, saw a polo match in England, bought a collection of mallets and balls, and upon returning to New York, bought a railroad car of Texan cow ponies. The first polo match in the United States was played on 6 May 1876 indoors at Dickel's Riding Academy, stationed at the corner of 39th Street and 5th Avenue. Later that same year Bennett established the Westchester Polo Club, and the first outdoor match played in the USA was held on the infield of the Jerome Park Racetrack.

The first international competition between the USA and England took place in August 1886. John Elliot Cowdin (an American 10-goaler) called the games between the Westchester Club and the Hurlingham Club the most important games in the history of polo. The first game of the two-game series was played on Wednesday 24 August at 4 p.m. By 3 o'clock the roads leading to the playing field were impassable. The clubhouse at Westchester was overflowing; people were sitting and standing on nearby hills to try to catch a glimpse of the game. Polo in the USA had never seen anything like it. The second game, held on the following Saturday, was even more crowded than the first. The Hurlingham team won the first game 10 to 4, and the second game 14 to 2.

The USA lost as a result of an ingenious development in team-play that the English had began using that same year: the back shot. The invention of the back shot sped up play, facilitated the transition from defence to offence and encouraged team-play and passing. The Americans were extremely bitter at their loss and a sign was posted outside the Westchester Club in Newport, Rhode Island stating, 'Any player making a backhand shot will be asked to leave the grounds.' However, after the initial sting of the loss to England, the Americans slowly started practising the back shot and were delighted at its effect on the game.

The United States Polo Association was founded in 1890. Over dinner one evening in March of that year, H.L. Herbert, John Cowdin, Thomas Hitchcock and a few other polo enthusiasts drafted the first set of American rules and created what is now known as the USPA. By June 1890, seven clubs had joined, and in no time a hundred handicaps had been awarded to amateur players, including future President 'Teddy' Roosevelt.

By the end of the nineteenth century, polo had really begun to take off in the USA. By 1894 the USPA had nineteen clubs in New England, with the furthest west being in St. Louis and the furthest south in Philadelphia.

Back in England, Winston Churchill was a prominent polo enthusiast and has given the sport some of the most notable quotes. He learned to play as a young cavalry officer in 1895. At that time he wrote to his mother asking for money to buy polo ponies, expressing a sentiment with which many polo players can sympathise: 'I cannot go on without any for more than a few days. Unless I give up the game, which would be dreadful.' Later stationed in India, he bought twenty-five ponies from another regiment and practised with his team daily, in blistering heat, determined to be the top team in the area. In 1899 they succeeded in winning the inter-regional tournament.

In *My Early Life*, an autobiography of his life up to 1902, he describes a game with the regent of Jodhpur:

Old Pertab, who loved polo next to war more than anything in the world, used to stop the game repeatedly and point out faults or possible improvements in our play and combination. 'Faster, faster, same like fly', he would shout to increase the speed of the game. The Jodhpore polo ground rises in great clouds of red dust when a game is in progress. These clouds carried to leeward of the strong breeze introduced a disturbing and somewhat dangerous complication. Turbaned figures emerged at full gallop from the dust-cloud, or the ball whistled out of it unexpectedly. It was difficult to follow the whole game, and one often had to play to avoid the dust-cloud.

He continued to play until the age of fifty-two, despite an injury to his right shoulder that forced him to ride with his mallet arm tied to his side. Later he advised parents:

> Don't give your son money. As far as you can afford it, give him horses. No one ever came to grief – except honourable grief – through riding horses. No hour of life is lost that is spent in the saddle. Young men have often been ruined through owning horses, or through backing horses, but never through riding them; unless of course they break their necks, which, taken at a gallop, is a very good death to die.

In 1891, J. Moray Brown wrote in the *Badminton Library of Sports and Pastimes*:

> angling teaches a man patience and self-control; (fox) hunting improves not only good horsemanship, but pluck and obser- vation; whilst shooting inculcates quickness of hand and eye coupled with endurance and the power of bearing fatigue. Football, cricket, rowing, rackets, tennis all bring to the front and encour- age qualities that are essentially manly; and perhaps no sport tends to combine all these lessons so much as polo, none makes a man more a man than this entrancing game, none fits him more for the sterner joys of war or enables him better to bear his part in the battle of life.

The final sentiment in this quotation was echoed years later when, as the United States prepared for the First World War, the Army Chief of Staff advised, 'US cavalry fighters are going to play polo in order to obtain poise in the saddle.'

Polo in the United States military actually began in 1896, at Fort Riley in Kansas. Cattle ponies were bought for $15 a head and teams were assembled. Not long after this, they hit the road and began friendly competition against teams at Fort Monroe in Virginia, Fort Sill in Oklahoma, Fort Bliss and Kelly Field in Texas, Fort Douglas in Utah and Fort Benning in Georgia. By 1902, the Army Polo Association had become affiliated to the USPA.

POLO FROM THE TWENTIETH CENTURY ONWARDS

The beginning of the twentieth century ushered in a golden era in polo. By the end of the nineteenth century, the height limit for ponies had been raised to 14.2 hands in both the USA and UK, which allowed a better line of ponies to be bred. In the USA, the tactic of hooking became legal in 1907. In 1908, in the USA, more than 20,000 fans attended an exhibition match at the Vermont State Fair. Games were regularly written up in New England newspapers and announced over the radio. In 1908, the USPA had thirty-seven clubs and 500 registered members. California joined the rosters in 1909. In 1910–11, handicapping became more universal, allowing better competition and encouraging international play.

As polo continued to gain in popularity, the fields became better maintained and sideboards were introduced in an attempt to keep the ball in play and encourage the fluidity of the game. Whereas players had previously used hunting saddles or military-style saddles, saddles specifically designed for polo were becoming available. These new polo saddles had a deep seat, with a high pommel and cantle for stability, but shorter stirrup leathers allowed the player to get up out of the saddle and twist during swings. Mallet design, material and quality improved. The British Army began applying their tactical training to the sport, defining roles and responsibilities for each position on the field.

Polo's popularity was spreading like wildfire. In the USA, in addition to being played across the main part of the continent, it was moving into territories such as the Philippines and Hawaii. In the south, ranch hands were even playing polo in Western saddles.

American polo at this time had its 'Big Four' heroes – Devereux Milburn, Harry Payne Whitney, and brothers Monty and Larry Waterbury. As a team, they never lost an international match. The Westchester

Cup matches against England of 1911 and 1913 went to the USA thanks to this dream team. The USA dominated England until Harry Payne Whitney's retirement from polo in 1914. The next two games against England were lost and the Cup moved back across the Atlantic.

Unfortunately for British polo, the Hurlingham Club grounds were occupied by Mounted Yeomanry squadrons throughout the First World War. Number One, the first and best of the polo fields on the grounds, was damaged by mortar rounds, and a hangar for The Royal Flying Corps was also constructed on the grounds. The combination of the war effort in general and this use of a key facility had a significant impact on the development of polo in the UK during this period, and for some time afterwards.

In the USA in 1915 the Indoor Polo Association was formed and in 1916 the USA abolished the height limits on ponies, a move followed in 1919 by the English. The National Polo Pony Society was formed that same year to 'stimulate and encourage the breeding of polo ponies'.

Prior to 1920, play was not stopped for penalties or fouls – these were, instead, awarded at the end of the chukka: ¼ point was deducted for a safety, ½ point for crossing the right of way, etc. Often, offenders were unaware that they had fouled until after the match, which made learning the sport that much more difficult. In 1920, though, the rules changed, and a new penalty system stopped play immediately after a foul. This improved the sport by encouraging stricter enforcement of the rules, creating more knowledgeable players and, by introducing the free shots from the 40- and 60-yard line, it made fouls much more detrimental to the offender.

After a series of matches in 1921, the USA brought the Westchester Cup back to America from England, and in 1924 more than 35,000 people watched the game on Long Island in which the USA beat the British 16-5. During this period, games were covered in newspapers and play-by-play reporting was broadcast on radio. In 1922 the National Polo Pony Society estimated that 63,000 ponies were played annually. Thomas Hitchcock, a celebrity athlete at the time, earned a 10-goal handicap, the highest possible ranking for a polo player, by the age of

A polo match from the 1920s era.

twenty-two. Women, also, began to take to the field, largely thanks to efforts by Mrs Thomas Hitchock Sr, and eventually they formed the US Women's Polo Association.

However, while polo was gaining widespread acceptance in the USA as a major-league sport, Argentina's reign as a world power in polo was just beginning. In the 1920s, Argentina began a breeding programme, crossing Argentine Thoroughbreds with the native Criollo horses, exploiting the speed of the Thoroughbred with the heart, hardiness, and handiness of the Criollo. In 1922, it was an Argentinean team that won the US Open. The pinnacle of Argentina's polo in that decade was winning the Olympic Gold Medal in 1924.

Back in the USA, by the 1930s, despite the nation's economy having crashed, the sport of polo was still on the ascendancy. Strategy advanced even more by applying tactics similar to those used in soccer. Passing the ball between players became the newest weapon on the polo field. The speed, the rapid change between offence and defence, and the fluidity of the positions made for a much more exciting game.

Several notable celebrities played as well: Leslie Howard, Will Rogers, Spencer Tracy, Johnny Mack Brown and Walt Disney to name a few. In 1935, the USPA claimed sixty-five clubs and roughly 2,500 players.

In an epic East meets West game, both number 3s on the opposing teams (Cecil Smith and Tommy Hitchcock) were at one point knocked unconscious, but later returned to finish the match. In the same game, Rube Williams' leg was broken in a ride-off. As a result, the USPA changed the rules to severely penalise rough play and ensure that injured players could be substituted if they were unable to play.

Internationally, in this period, the USA won every match (1930, 1936 and 1939) of the Westchester Cup against Great Britain. Crowds of 40,000 gathered in Rhode Island at the Meadow Brook Polo Club. The USA was even dominating competitions against Argentina, until 1936, when Argentina, fresh from winning at the Olympics, defeated the USA in the Cup of the Americas.

Throughout the Second World War, the grounds of the Hurlingham Polo Club in England were once again pressed into service for the war effort, being turned over to the government for agricultural use – and they were built over afterwards. The sport was officially suspended during the war. (In 1952, however, the Hurlingham Polo Association started up again at Cowdray, in Sussex.) What happened at Hurlingham was an indication of widespread socio-economic consequences of the war and these consequences were reinforced by various broader technological and social changes. Military reliance on the horse had started to diminish just before the First World War, when motorcycles and jeeps proved faster and more resilient. The Second World War signalled the end of the use of horses in the military almost universally. Although the US military continued to use polo as a means to train and harden officers until this war, eventually, the military barns were closed and the horses sold. The remount depots also closed, causing a marked decline in the number of mounts available for the sport.

This disbanding of the remount depots, coupled with the stresses war and a general change of focus for the United States, meant that polo saw a sharp decline in this era. By the end of the 1940s, the USPA only had about forty-eight clubs (none of which were Army or Collegiate) and, during this period, could only claim four 10-goalers: Stewart Ingelart, Mark Phipps, Cecil Smith and Tommy Hitchcock Jr. Unfortunately, in 1944, Hitchcock died in a crash-landing in a military test aircraft in Wiltshire, England.

During the 1940s Mexico, on the other hand, had a polo-loving president: Manuel Ávila Camacho. In 1941 a tournament called the Camacho Cup was inaugurated in Mexico City and here, the USA achieved considerable success, winning all three games that year and dominating the subsequent years up to 1946. However, a Mexican team composed only of the Gracida family redeemed Mexican pride by winning the 1946 US Open at Meadow Brook. In 1949 the first USPA rule book (the 'Blue Book') was published.

In the 1950s, following the constraints of the war years, polo began a steady re-emergence in America and the UK. In the USA, the famed polo grounds at Meadow Brook were sold after the last US Open to be played there was held in 1953. The 'headquarters' of US polo then moved to the Oak Brook Polo Club in Hinsdale, Illinois. Polo also began to flourish in other states such as Florida, Texas and Oklahoma. By mid-decade, the Indoor Polo Association had joined forces with the USPA and, thanks to efforts by USPA Chairman Devereux Milburn, developing and supporting young players became a new initiative. Collegiate, scholastic and indoor games were promoted as excellent tools for teaching a new generation of polo players. Indoor polo in particular used fewer ponies and opened up the sport to more people who could afford it.

In the 1960s, polo in the United States really gathered momentum. In 1963 the US Open returned to the West Coast. The Polo School Committee was created in 1966, and the Polo Training Foundation (PTF) opened in 1967 thanks to a generous donation by the Hickox family of Long Island. Again, though, Stewart Iglehart, Robert Skene and Cecil Smith remained the only 10-goal players.

The Cup of the Americas series was started up again, taking place in 1966 and 1969. The American team comprised Northrup Knox (Captain), Dr William Linfoot, Roy and Harold Barry and, in 1969, Bennie Gutierrez. Sick ponies and a harrowing plane trip plagued the American team on its journey to Argentina in 1966, but both series were lost.

In 1966, the Houston Polo Association was formed and indoor polo was played in the Houston Astrodome. Collegiate polo was now back in full swing. An ivy-league rivalry struck up between Yale and Cornell when, in 1967, the Orthwein twin Steve's team (Yale) beat his brother Peter's team (Cornell) in the Intercollegiate Championship.

The 1970s saw the emergence of greater female interest in polo in the USA. In 1973, Elizabeth Dailey, Sue Sally Hale, Virginia Merchant, Jorie Butler Richardson and six others were the first women to be assigned USPA handicaps. It didn't take long before women were taking the sport by storm. In 1976, the first all-woman's tournament at California's Carmel Valley Riding and Polo Center took place. In 1979, the first US Women's Handicap was played.

This decade also saw the development to the corporate and professional polo we know today. America in particular embraced corporate sponsorship of high-goal polo teams, and the professionals it attracted. USPA membership increased as professionals of all levels (some professionals are low-goal players) and from all corners of the globe became more readily available. Subsequently, such an influx of high-goal polo professionals engendered an increase in larger, more elaborate polo clubs. However, despite this progress, there were no American 10-goalers during in the 1970s.

The 1980s saw even more corporate sponsorship, bigger purses, and more high-goal talent attracted to the USA from around the world. These professional players replaced the talented amateurs from leading polo families. Team sponsors paid for talented professionals, top-quality ponies, and vied for the prize money the major polo clubs offered. Companies like Rolex, Cartier, Johnny Walker, Cadillac, etc. were sponsoring teams and tournaments across the nation. This only helped to promote the image of polo as a high-class, expensive sport. Many wealthy businessmen picked up the game as a status symbol, and used the sport as a means to promote their business.

This change in dynamic from teams made up entirely of talented amateurs to teams founded on one or two higher-goal professionals mixed with less experienced players created a unique challenge for the USPA to handicap the players better. The -1 and -2 handicaps were added in the 1980s to further level the playing field. To complement this change, there was focus on improving umpiring as well.

The changing dynamic applied to ponies, as well as players. Whereas, earlier in the century, ponies were being bred and trained in the western states to supply the demand from polo players in the east, by now Argentina and Chile were supplying their top-quality Criollo/Thoroughbred crosses to the whole of the United States.

During the 1980s, USPA membership reached an all-time high. By the end of the decade, there were 3,042 players, 208 clubs and 25 colleges and universities playing the sport. Women also began to play a significant role in the sport: not only were they playing in colleges and at tournaments, they were also working as instructors, team managers, pony trainers and even club managers.

Although Tommy Wayman was the only American-born 10-goaler of the 1980s, the Mexican Gracida brothers, Memo and Carlos, also 10-goal, were considered to be US players.

In 1997, after seventeen years of planning, the National Museum of Polo and Hall of Fame finally opened at Lake Worth, Florida. Although the Polo Training Foundation continued to have success with youth programmes around the United States, the total USPA membership reached a plateau at around 3,000 members.

Today, Argentina is still the Mecca for polo *aficionados*. The country continually produces top-quality players and ponies, and there are regularly crowds of 30,000 fans attending major games.

The sport itself is unique. It is a team sport, in which success is reliant not just on human teammates, but on each player's relationship with an individual animal teammate. The connection between pony and rider, the excitement, the speed, the difficulty, the challenge, and the camaraderie will secure polo's future. Now, more than ever, the sport is accessible to an ever-widening range of people, regardless of age, sex, or economic status. In the USA, programmes such as 'Work to Ride' allow impoverished inner-city kids a chance to work in stables in return for learning the sport of polo, and South Africa has a broadly similar programme called 'Poloafrice'.

(Having talked about accessibility, I should explain at this point that polo always has to be played with the mallet in the right hand. This is not because of some evil conspiracy against left-handers but because having a left-handed player converging head-on with a right-hander when both were trying to play the ball would be a recipe for carnage. In some

More young players are coming into the sport today.

sports, such as golf, it is not unknown for natural left-handers to play right-handed – or vice versa – so this is something that might be worth investigating with regard to polo.)

Today polo is played in nearly eighty countries across the world, with over half of the world's players being based in Argentina, England, and the United States. Because of the widespread appeal of polo, an internationally organised effort exists to promote the sport. The Federation of International Polo (FIP) has organised international tournaments in an effort to return the sport to the Olympics. In addition to year-round international tournaments, clinics and events, the World Cup is played every three years. The FIP has done tremendous work creating and drafting an international set of rules, and brainstorming how the sport would work in the Olympics (pony pools, etc.).

There are many studies, theories and reports on how the growth of polo as a sport can be promoted and encouraged. The main pillar is exposing the sport to a larger audience. Whereas, in the recent past, polo was played primarily by movie stars and royalty, nowadays it can be played by nearly anyone. The best thing we can do as *aficionados* and fans of the sport is to share it with everyone we can.

CHAPTER TWO

Equipment

TACK

All of the equipment you will use on your pony has been developed over many years to optimise communication, comfort and safety for both you and the pony. In times past, many indigenous people, including Native Americans, used a rope bridle (a loose loop of rope slipped into the horse's mouth) and rode bareback. In time, metal bits were introduced to enhance communication and a saddle was introduced to add comfort and stability for the rider and the mount. Nowadays we have thousands of different types of bits, made in all shapes, of all kinds of metals, and different styles of saddles have been developed for different uses.

I recommend buying used equipment in good condition. There will always be a breaking-in process with leather and similar materials which could reduce efficiency. Stirrup leathers, for example, should be switched from side to side frequently to avoid uneven stretching of the left one alone during mounting. Make periodic inspection of your equipment, as well, in order to detect loose stitching or any other defect as soon as possible.

A full set of tack in place.

Bridle and its fitting

A basic bridle consists of the headpiece, which goes behind the pony's ears and connects on either side to the cheekpieces; the browband, which goes over the pony's forehead, in front of his ears; the throatlatch and the noseband. The bridle is a key part of your equipment since it provides the means of attaching the bit and the reins. The materials and care of your bridle are extremely important, as is the fit. In addition to the other elements being adjustable so as to be both comfortable to the pony and secure, the cheekpieces must be capable of maintaining the bit at the appropriate height in the pony's mouth.

When fitting your bridle, always make sure you can slide your hand vertically through the throatlatch, and that there is plenty of room for

opposite page A team's tack, ready and waiting.

A correctly fitted bridle, with drop noseband and gag snaffle.

your pony to arch his neck and breathe properly. This strap is just a safety strap if the bridle should ever happen to come over your pony's ears (which could happen, as it did to me, as a consequence of foul tactics by an opponent), in which case the throatlatch will keep it on long enough for you to stop and dismount. The browband should lie flat against the pony's forehead. Make sure it is not too short and thus so tight that it pinches the headpiece or brings it forward. The noseband should be snug, but loose enough so that you can fit two fingers between the leather and the pony's easily.

The drop noseband

In the section on Bit Selection (see below) I acknowledge that polo is a fast and furious sport, and that if over-harsh rein aids are used, this can lead to ponies learning various evasions. These evasions may include throwing up the head and opening the mouth. If combined with bunching up the tongue and pressing it against the bit, or slipping the tongue over the bit, the bit itself will be rendered useless. A drop noseband is designed to prevent the pony from opening his mouth enough to accomplish this.

Gag bits will often be used in conjunction with a drop noseband. Unlike a cavesson noseband (the standard type, which fastens round the pony's nose above the mouth), the drop is a separate loop of leather that fastens on the *outside* of the bit, *around* the pony's mouth. This is intended to prevent the pony from opening his mouth and evading the rein aids. It should be fitted very carefully so that it goes underneath the chin groove but rests high enough on the nose so that it runs over the nasal bone, not over the soft part of the nostrils. Despite its intended purpose of preventing the pony from opening his mouth and evading the rein aids, it should not be fitted *too* tight – as with a cavesson noseband, you should be able to slide two fingers between the leather and the pony's nose easily.

Bit fitting

It may seem a little odd to discuss the fitting of the bit before talking about bit selection, but there are two reasons for doing so. First, as just touched upon, the bridle itself must be of a size and design that will accommodate correct adjustment of the chosen bit. Secondly, in some cases the conformation of a pony's mouth may be one of the factors that influence the type of bit that works best for that individual. Further to this, if at all possible, it is recommended that each pony should have their own bridle and their own bit, so that you know without doubt that the fit is correct. Bits are relatively inexpensive and will last your entire polo career, so they are a smart investment.

The fitting of the bit is a hotly debated topic and every professional will have their own standards, and every pony will have his preferences. No two riders are the same; no two ponies are the same. Mouths can vary in the length of the bars (the space between the incisors and the molars), the thickness of the tongue and the height of the mouth between the tongue and palate. Also, if there is any scarring from a previous injury, or broken or cracked teeth, special consideration needs to be given to these issues.

These points aside, the three main concerns when fitting a bit are how high it sits in the mouth, the width of the mouthpiece and the diameter of the mouthpiece.

In showing and showjumping, bits are usually fastened high enough in the mouth that one, two or three wrinkles appear on the horse's cheeks. For polo, I prefer to adjust the bit low enough in the pony's mouth so that no wrinkles appear, but high enough that it does not hit the pony's teeth. This lets the pony 'pick up' the bit with his tongue and carry it where he finds it comfortable. This increases responsiveness and communication. Imagine the difference between a steering column in your car where the power steering is well lubricated and the column fits well, and a steering column without power-steering fluid that's been jammed into a tight fit. On the other hand, a bit that hangs *too low* in the pony's mouth can encourage him to slip his tongue on top of the bit, making it ineffective.

Whatever the case concerning the height of the bit, the golden rule is that when you apply pressure to the reins, the bit should be able to move against the pony's lips and that he does not show signs of discomfort. If the bit is fixed too high in the mouth, the constant rubbing will desensitise the corners of the mouth. It will also not give the pony the release he is looking for when he obeys the commands. If the rider pulls on the bit to stop, and the bit is fixed high in the mouth, the pony will continue to feel pressure after he has stopped.

Concerning the width of a bit, the average width used in polo is 5–5½in, but the basic rule of thumb is that, correctly placed in your pony's mouth, the bit should only have ¼–½in of play between the lips and the bit ring. A bit that is too wide will slide through the pony's mouth when pressure is applied, see-sawing across the pony's tongue and perhaps bruising the bars of the mouth. In the case of a jointed bit, it will also produce a nutcracker effect in which the joint could hit the roof of the mouth, causing extreme pain. On the other hand, a bit that is too small will pinch the pony's lips and cause callusing or cuts.

To measure a specific pony, insert a wooden dowel or piece of string/ baling twine in the mouth where the bit would sit and mark the edges of the pony's lips.

Regarding the diameter of the mouthpiece, this is only one factor in its effect on the pony, since actual design and materials are also significant. However, diameter is still highly significant, and not always fully understood. A thin mouthpiece always has the mechanical potential to be harsher than a thicker one, which will spread the pressure more easily, and a very thin mouthpiece will act like a wire cheese-cutter on a pony's tongue. However, this does not mean that it is always good practice to use a thick mouthpiece because, in a small mouth, such a mouthpiece can be crowding and uncomfortable.

One very important point to note, applicable to all equestrian disciplines, is that an incorrectly fitted bit that causes pain for long enough time can completely undo any horse's or pony's training. I once acquired a mare named La Loca, a beautiful, delicate, well-bred Thoroughbred. She was given to me free, because every time someone tried to ride her she would flip over backwards on top of them. I rode her successfully for years afterwards as long as I never put a bit in her mouth. I can only assume she was ridden one day with a bit that caused her so much pain that she threw herself on her back in an attempt to run away. Once she learned that trick, she had a way to get every rider off her back.

Bit selection

It is said that there is a key to every pony's mouth; meaning there is a bit out there that fits the pony perfectly. That said, two different riders may require two different bits to get the best out of the same pony. One rider may get the best out of a pony with a simple snaffle, while another rider may feel that this bit does not offer the optimum level of communication, and another bit is required.

When choosing a bit, look at what the people around you are using. If one player seems to have seamless connection with their pony and the pony is going well, relaxed, and there is good communication between the two, ask what bit that player is using, and why. If at all possible, ride a high-goal pony: one who has been impeccably trained, to get a feeling of the level of communication obtainable if everything is working well. If you have reason to believe that one of the less common bits may help your situation, ask around to see if a fellow polo player, or even a rider from another discipline, has experience of such a bit and will let you try it (if it fits).

Here is a story from my own experience to show how important the choice of correct bit can be (in this instance, it was a case of simplest is best). Once when I was playing in Chile, I had been riding the same

Two polo ponies waiting for the game, showing different bitting. The pony on the left is wearing a snaffle with draw reins; the pony on the right is wearing a Pelham.

little Criollo gelding the entire week and was in love. To this day, he is probably the best pony I've ever sat on. He went in a simple snaffle with a metal curb with rollers and only one rein, but I felt as though I could place him on a penny. The last game we played, the groom accidently put a Pelham in his mouth and we were instantly taken out of the game for the first chukka. All communication was lost, every time I touched the bit; it was too hard on him and he resisted instantly, offended by the pressure. But that taught me an extremely important lesson: a good pony can be ruined by the wrong bit. I wonder how many ponies would play better if only we used the right bit.

One point we must acknowledge is that polo requires repeated hard stops and turns. If the bit is severe or the hand is too harsh, the pony will find a way to evade the pressure of the bit. Many will do so either by lifting their head, slipping their tongue over the bit, grabbing the bit, or tucking their nose to their chest. A very common evasion among polo ponies is to throw their head up, tighten down their back and let their hind end drag out. While this form of evasion is commonplace on the polo field, it is detrimental to the pony's well-being. A pony who stops with his head in the air over an extended period will start showing symptoms of a sore back.

Heavy-handed use of the reins will cause a pony to throw up his head and evade the bit.

While slipping the tongue over the bit and grabbing the bit are not necessarily detrimental to the pony, they are a danger to the rider. The bit becomes useless and the rider may no longer have control of the pony.

The pony who tucks his nose into his chest is reacting differently from the one who puts his head in the air, but it remains the case that he is evading the bit. While, in some respects, tucking the nose in may be preferable to throwing the head up, it can still cause physical damage and thus requires correction.

There are three major types of bits used on the polo field: the simple gag and the double gag (from the family of snaffles), and curb bits. All bits that have movable parts next to the horse's lips should have bit guards (sometimes called 'biscuits' in UK, or *donuts* in USA), to prevent the horse's lips getting pinched during play. Up until around the 1940s, nickel was the preferred material for making bits. Nowadays, the majority are made out of stainless steel, but bits can be found in copper, sweet iron (cold rolled steel) or a combination of metals. The idea behind these alternative metals is that they encourage salivation in the horse's mouth, creating a lubricated and more communicative surface. Bits can also be obtained in plastic or rubber, which do not rust and are thought to be gentler than metal bits. With a curb or a gag bit, the longer the curb or the bigger the ring on the gag, the more pressure it will inflict on the horse's poll. Every bit, in the wrong hands, can be painful to the horse but, in the right hands, even the most severe bit can be a delicate tool.

Bits of the snaffle family

Plain snaffle

The most widely used bit across any discipline is the snaffle. It is the least interfering, the least complicated, and the most readily accepted by a young (USA *green*) horse. A simple snaffle uses direct pressure rather than leverage on the pony's mouth. A snaffle can either have a jointed mouthpiece or a straight bar. The snaffle affects several parts of the pony's mouth: the tongue, bars and lips. Snaffles are preferred for training and exercise where communication is less demanding.

Most disciplines that rely heavily on snaffles do not use a curb chain/strap in conjunction with such a bit. This device is either a chain or a strap of leather that runs from the bit cheekpieces underneath the chin. Curb chains/straps attached to bits that impart leverage add pressure to the chin, but a curb strap on a snaffle can be used to keep the bit from sliding out of one side of the mouth.

A well-fitted snaffle.

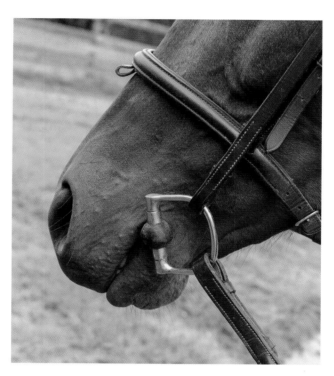

Simple gag

The simple gag is just that. It consists of a single bar, jointed in the middle to allow it to follow the curvature of the pony's tongue. There is generally a fabric or leather piece that runs from the bridle cheekpieces through the middle of the bit ring and out the bottom to connect to the second rein. This gag portion acts as a lever and, when pressure is applied, it cantilevers against the pony's mouth and applies pressure to the poll, just behind the ears. This encourages the pony to lower his head as he slows down. As mentioned earlier, a thin mouthpiece is more severe than a thick one. You can also buy simple gags with twisted mouthpieces, in which the metal mouthpiece looks as if it's been twisted into a corkscrew. This increases the effect over the pony's tongue and is less severe than a double gag, but more severe than a snaffle. There are also a difference in severity between a fast twist and a slow twist.

Double gag/Barry gag

In a double gag, or Barry gag, there are two metal pieces over the pony's tongue, articulating at offset joints. These joints fold the bit around the tongue and the dual mouthpieces double the pressure delivered to the tongue and cheeks, adding extra strength to the rein aids. Just as in the simple gag, a double gag bit can have a twist in it as well.

below left A simple gag.

below right A double gag.

Curb bits

Curb bits have a shank, a secondary piece coming off the mouthpiece to which the bottom rein attaches, creating leverage. Leverage bits not only apply pressure directly to the mouth, but also use a fulcrum action to apply pressure behind the ears. In a double bridle (see page 45), which uses both a small snaffle mouthpiece (called a bradoon) and a curb mouthpiece, the top rein that attaches directly to the bradoon should be marginally shorter than the bottom rein, which attaches to the curb. In a Pelham (see below), which is a single bit, there is a similar arrangement whereby the shorter top rein attaches to the main bit ring, while the bottom rein attaches to the shank part of the bit. In both cases, the top rein should engage the pony first, with leverage from the bottom rein

A Pelham bit – a type of curb.

THE COMPLETE GUIDE TO **POLO**

reinforcing this action as and when necessary. The length of the shank determines the severity of the leverage applied to the back of the poll and chin; the longer the shank, the more pressure.

Curb bits usually also have a curb chain/strap that goes underneath the pony's chin, also producing leverage against the chin, to induce a greater stopping effect. A chain is obviously more intense in its action than leather, but if your pony has delicate skin under the chin, a leather strap is a welcome alternative. Alternatively, chains can be run through a rubber sleeve, to make their presence and action more comfortable. When fitting a bit with a curb chain, you should be able to slide two fingers width-wise between the pony's jaw and the chain. Another way to judge the adjustment and effectiveness is to pull back gently on the shankpiece. The chain should engage when the shanks are at 45 degrees from the vertical.

For training purposes, a curb bit can be used with a single rein, either attached to the mouthpiece alone, or to the shanks alone. Obviously, a bit with the rein attached to the mouthpiece will only engage the mouthpiece; a rein attached to the shank will only engage the shank.

Pelhams

The Pelham is a type of curb bit that is usually fitted with the mouthpiece placed lower in the mouth than with other patterns, avoiding wrinkles in the lips. The lower the bit is placed, however, the more severe its action, since the lower part of the bars of the mouth are thinner and more delicate. In addition to the mouth pressure, a Pelham can apply pressure behind the poll. The mouthpiece can be a straight bar, or have a port (arch) in the middle, or be jointed.

As you can visualise, a pony's tongue is not flat, but more rounded. Genuinely straight-bar Pelhams do not give any room for tongue relief, but provide constant tongue pressure. While this may not bother some ponies, others may be annoyed by it, or even interpret it as a signal. To avoid this, a 'mullen' mouthpiece is a solid bar with a curve in it, allowing the tongue some room and placing even pressure on the bars and tongue. These mouthpieces are sometimes made out of plastic or rubber.

In a way similar to a mullen mouth, the idea behind a ported mouth-piece is that, if a pony has a large, rounded tongue, the arch will relieve some of the pressure on it. However, if the port is too high, or the roof of the pony's mouth low, the port will actually press against the palate when engaged, causing extreme pain.

Unlike jointed snaffles, which are relatively mild, when the shanks are engaged on a jointed Pelham they apply pressure on the bars, and the joint can roll forward and, as with too high a port, potentially dig into the roof of the mouth.

above left A ported Pelham.

above right A straight-bar Pelham.

Double bridles

Double bridles are not commonly found on the polo field but could be useful training tools. As mentioned earlier, they have two mouthpieces, a snaffle (traditionally called a bradoon) *and* a curb bit. Often used in classical dressage, they are designed to fine-tune control of both lateral and forward movement. For example, the double bridle allows you to influence one side of the pony's mouth with direct rein pressure while still having the option of employing a curb rein. In a normal curb bit, pressure on one rein will spread the communication throughout the mouth, and could produce a twisting effect, causing the curb chain to pinch. In a double bridle, the snaffle bit (bradoon) will communicate direct pressure while the curb bit will add pressure to the bars, chin and the poll. The curb bit will also encourage vertical flexion, yielding at the poll and thus encouraging the pony to go with an arched rather than 'hollow' (inverted) neck. While this rounded outline of the neck is far from the whole story in producing collection, it does help encourage the rounding of the rest of the spinal process, thus making it easier for the pony's hind legs to engage actively beneath his body.

It is important to note here that if the pony is already carrying his head where you want it, the curb rein should be loose and the snaffle rein alone used to direct him.

Bitless bridles/hackamores

Many polo ponies start their training in a bitless bridle or hackamore. The word 'hackamore' comes from the Spanish word *jáquima* meaning halter. While not used on the field, these are great training tools to use off the field or during the off season. They are in effect a normal bridle with a thicker noseband and no bit attachment. They can be as simple as a halter with a lead line around the pony's neck, or a special attachment to a regular bridle, complete with shanks and a curb.

It's easy to assume that a bitless bridle is gentler than a bitted bridle but this is not the case. A pony's face has very thin skin full of nerve endings, and pinching the skin between the bone and a strap can be more painful than anything in the mouth, therefore fitting and use should be done with due care. The hackamore I used on my mare La Loca, mentioned earlier, was a simple English bridle with a thick, leather noseband.

A halter-type hackamore.

Some polo ponies will become sour towards the end of the season. They are tired, burning-out, possibly sore. They can start to ignore the bit. At this point, you can either put a stronger bit in their mouths, or begin exercising them in a hackamore. The latter teaches them to listen to pressure; to give to pressure. Horses in all disciplines are trained to give in to pressure, to move away from pressure. Using a hackamore reminds them of this. It heightens their sensitivity without abusing their mouths.

Reins and associated tack

Standard reins

The majority of polo bridles will have two sets of reins, an upper and lower set. Most reins are made of leather, but they can be found with rubber grips, or entirely of rubber and plastic as well. The rubber and plastic reins handle water and sweat well without deterioration and can be easily hosed off without worry. Leather reins require cleaning and conditioning but I find they feel better in the hand.

Generally speaking, the bottom, or shank rein, will be thicker than the top, snaffle rein. This makes them easier to distinguish in the middle of a game when you have to rearrange your reins.

Reins should be inspected prior to mounting before every game. If one were to break in the middle of a match it could mean a complete loss of control over the pony and turn into a very dangerous situation.

Draw reins

A pony who stops correctly will tuck his hind end underneath him, lift his forehand, but keep his head and neck down and relaxed. However, the demands of polo are such that it is not uncommon for ponies to develop the habit of inverting their back, throwing their head up in the air and bracing their mouth against the bit when stopping. This hollows out their back, forces their hind legs far out from underneath them, overdevelops the muscles on the underside of the neck and is detrimental to joints, muscles and other tissues. The physical stresses involved also make it harder for the pony to be relaxed mentally. Stopping in this way is just like a kid, running flat-out down a hill with no control, legs just barely keeping up enough to keep him upright. If not controlled, it's dangerous and usually only ends one way.

Draw reins are often fitted to polo ponies to try to prevent them from stopping incorrectly. They run from the saddle billets where the girth attaches, through the rings of the bit and to the rider's hand. This arrangement applies downward pressure to the bit when the rider applies a rein aid.

A lot of players will play every pony in draw reins, but they can be overused. A pony who overreacts to draw reins will begin to tuck his chin into his chest, which is also not desirable. The pony's forehead and nasal bone should never flex beyond the vertical.

Standing martingale

This is another piece of tack designed to prevent the pony from lifting his head too high. As mentioned, if a pony throws his head up too high, he is evading the effects of the bit. In addition to being dangerous, this overdevelops incorrect muscles and can cause damage to the back and hindquarters. Additionally, if the rider is in the middle of a swing and bent over the pony's neck, the pony can actually break the rider's nose with a toss of his head.

The standing martingale, or tie-down, that most polo players use is a thick leather strap that runs from the noseband of the bridle, down the pony's chest, between the forelegs, and attaches to the girth. A thinner leather band wraps around the pony's neck just in front of the saddle and keeps the martingale tucked up against the pony so that stray mallets do not get tangled up in it.

Draw reins run from the girth, through the bit's rings and back to the rider's hand.

When fitting a martingale, make sure the neckstrap is tight enough to keep the martingale strap as close against the neck as possible. The martingale strap itself should be loose enough to not restrict the natural movement of the neck; it is just there to prevent the pony from raising his head too high. When on the pony, you should be able to bring the martingale strap up along the side of his neck and it should just reach to the jugular groove of the neck.

Saddle and associated tack

Saddle

An appropriate saddle is extremely important for horse and rider in any discipline. Polo saddles are close-contact, forward-seat (girth set back) with a deep seat and large flaps without any knee or calf rolls. They are designed to provide maximum comfort, maximum safety and maximum contact.

An ill-fitting saddle can permanently damage the nerves and muscles in a pony's shoulders and back. It can also cause pressure points so severe as to produce bald spots or areas where only white hair will grow. A point to bear in mind when buying a polo pony is to check for these spots and double-check that no lasting damage was done.

When fitting a saddle, place it as far forward on the pony as possible and slide it back so that it fits naturally where the withers blend into the back. Be sure, though, that it does not interfere with the natural movement of the long muscle of the shoulder. The weight of the rider should be supported by the broad muscles that run along the pony's ribs. Check that it does not go further down the back than the last ribs. Although described as close-contact, polo saddles are designed so that there should be three to four fingers' width between the bottom of the pommel and the pony's withers with the weight of a rider in the

A polo saddle in place. This modern form is very different from the saddles used in earlier eras. Padding in some form – in this case, a folded blanket – is used to protect both the pony and the saddle.

stirrups. Ideally, when viewed from the side and with a rider in the seat, the pommel and cantle (front and back) of the saddle should be level. With the saddle on the pony's back, run your hands underneath the saddle and make sure there are no bumps or ripples or folds, and that no one part places more pressure on the back than another. Also, flip your hands over and check the panels visually. They should be even, symmetrical, and full. Another good test for a saddle's fit is to check the sweat mark it leaves on the pony's back after a chukka. Even with a saddle pad, there will be a distinct saddle-sized sweat mark on the pony's back. If the sweat mark is only on one side of the back, or is only there in parts, you know the saddle is not putting even pressure on the back.

The tree of the saddle should be taken into consideration as well; it must be of a width that matches the pony's back. A narrow tree will pinch a pony's withers and the delicate tendons and nerves that run along the withers. Run your hands along your pony's back with the saddle on to be sure the tree is wide enough. Be aware, also, that *too* wide a tree could potentially reduce the weight-bearing area and even put pressure on the spine.

Some ponies will have very pronounced, sloping withers, while others will have nearly no withers at all. For the pony with pronounced withers, where the pommel sits drastically higher than the cantle, it is possible to buy pads of varying thickness (rear riser pads) to suit each individual's needs. For the pony who has no withers to speak of, a non-slip pad can be used underneath the saddle pad to keep the saddle from sliding.

Polo saddles tend to have flatter seats than those for other disciplines to allow the rider to stand and twist during the swing or a ride-off. Although flat, the seat tends to be deep, with a high cantle. Make sure that, when you are in the saddle, the lowest part is evenly between the pommel and the cantle, so your weight is balanced in the middle of the saddle. The flaps are long and flat, giving the optimum balance between protection and maintaining the best degree of contact with the pony. Your legs need to swing around a lot and padding would interfere with this motion.

A saddle that is the wrong size for the rider will be the difference between an effective player and someone off their game. Most of the polo saddles you'll see on the field are between 17 and 19 inches from front to back. Obviously, with men and women, young and old, and people of all sizes playing, you can imagine that not everyone's backside is going to fit snugly in 17–19 inches of saddle. Note that, although the saddle fitting the rider is important, purchasing a saddle for the rider's comfort should not come at the expense of the pony's comfort. Saddle fit should take into account both the rider's and the pony's comfort for optimum performance.

The lowest part of the saddle should be the narrowest part of the seat, where the rider's seat bones would rest. This helps put the rider in balance over the correct part of the pony. When the rider is seated in the centre of the saddle, it should be possible to place a hand's width in front of and behind the rider's pelvis. A saddle that is too small for the rider will be uncomfortable and will push them either too far forward or too far backwards. On the other hand, a saddle that is too big does not provide enough support and will cause the rider to slide around in the seat. Most polo saddles are still designed with the pelvic structure of a man in mind. If you are a female, and you find a saddle that fits you well, try to replicate it, or find the manufacturer and order the same pattern.

With a rider in the stirrups, the saddle should never leave the pony's back. When the rider is rising to the trot (USA *posting*), or cantering, the saddle should remain still. This way, the weight of the rider in the stirrups is actually distributed along the entire length of the saddle. If the stirrups put all the weight forward on the saddle, the pony will have extremely sore withers.

The positioning of the stirrup leathers (derived from the position of the stirrup bars on the saddle tree) is very important because of the influence this has on the rider's position. The rider's hip angle and knee angle should be open, but the heel should be easily brought underneath the hip during motion. If the stirrup leathers are attached to the saddle too far forward, they will force the rider's legs forward and the rider's

Rider's leg position.

weight to fall back onto the rear of the buttocks. If the stirrup leathers are too far back, they will push the rider's weight forwards. When buying a saddle, make sure that the safety catches (USA *stirrup releases*) are smooth and quick to release. In polo, it is common for a rider's leg to kick out backwards and away from the pony when reaching far for a hook or during a swing, hence the safety catches should remain in the 'up' position, requiring a significant amount of pressure to push the release into the 'down' position. That said, if you should fall off, and your foot gets caught in the stirrup, you *do* want the stirrup leather to be able to able to release from the saddle.

Before and after a game, when using a new saddle or trying out a saddle to buy, run your fingers along the pony's muscles on either side of the spine. Put a decent amount of pressure behind this. If the pony twitches the muscles or drops away from your hands, his back hurts.

Saddle pads

Saddle pads go between the pony and the saddle to protect the leather from sweat, add cushioning and protect the pony from rubs. They can be rectangular polo saddle pads, fitted pads, or a folded blanket. Some polo players prefer not to use pads, trying to get a closer feel to the pony. As long as care is taken that the saddle fits properly and the pony does not need extra padding, and that the saddle is wiped off well after each match, this is acceptable.

When using a saddle pad, I like to place it so that at least 4 inches sits in front of the saddle. Make sure there is also at least the same length behind the saddle. After placing the saddle on top of the pad, I like to pull the pad up to meet the saddle above the withers. I find the saddle then seems to sit more snugly on the withers, instead of being propped on top of a taut saddle pad.

Stirrup leathers and irons

On polo saddles, the stirrup leathers are thicker than on other English saddles because of the wear and tear they receive. Before every match, check the stitching to prevent any mid-game breaks. Also, every couple weeks, switch the left and right stirrups and leathers. Otherwise, constantly mounting from the left side means that the left leather will stretch more than the right one.

Stirrup 'irons' are no longer made of iron, but of stainless steel instead. The stirrup irons on polo saddles are larger and thicker than irons on other saddles. The wider tread is more comfortable for the way polo players ride. Polo players tend to ride with the foot 'home' in the stirrup, or with the tread directly underneath the arch of the foot rather than the ball of the foot. The bridge of the iron is also larger to allow the boot to slide out in the event of a fall.

Some stirrup irons are hinged in the middle, ideally to facilitate putting your weight in your heel, but also to release the foot during a fall. Another type of iron, designed to allow the foot to come free, will have a curve or relief on the outside bridge of the iron. Some irons have

A polo stirrup iron.

rubber soles wedged in the treads, but these are not commonly used in polo because they tend to fall out during ride-offs.

In polo, there are generally two different styles of stirrup leather length; shorter or longer. Shorter leathers allow more mobility. The forward seat was first used by light cavalry, allowing riders to twist their upper body in any direction to shoot, use swords, etc., and to use hips, knees and ankles as shock absorbers. Similarly, in polo, when you stand in the stirrups to perform a swing, you need to be able to get high enough out of the saddle so that you can rotate your hips freely. Also, the faster a pony goes, the more forward his centre of gravity may move. To maintain balance over the pony's centre of gravity at speed, the polo player must ride more forward in the saddle and hence, have shorter leathers. *Too short*, though, and it will be like trying to stand after sitting on a couch.

Longer stirrup leathers, however, allow more stability and control, which can be an advantage if you're on a pony you're unsure about, or one who has a tendency to buck or crow hop. *Too long*, though, and you won't be able to rise out of the saddle effectively. You'll notice that a rider with stirrup leathers that are too long seems to be 'left behind' the motion of the pony. When the pony's back flexes and extends through the stride of the canter, the rider seems to be pushed and pulled against the motion, not with it. Long stirrup leathers also equals straight legs. When the angles of the leg (hip, knee, and ankle) are open or straight, there is not a lot of room for the leg to absorb the movement of the pony.

As a general rule, though, the bottom of the stirrup iron should hit just underneath your ankle bone when your legs hang relaxed in the saddle. Ideally, the stirrup should be underneath the ball of the foot, allowing the heel to drop below it, accepting all of the rider's weight. This allows the ankle to flex and absorb the motion of the pony.

Girth

Girths come in many different shapes, sizes and varieties. They should be cleaned daily and checked frequently for loose stitching and wear. Most girths will be made of leather or cotton, but neoprene girths used extensively in the jumping disciplines have started to find favour on the polo field. Neoprene girths require little maintenance, just soap and water to clean, and are less likely to slip, especially with a sweaty pony.

Girth billets are especially important. Billets can be either two individual straps, of elastic or leather, or one longer strap with two buckles called an equaliser. This equaliser is a movable strap that lets one billet ride slightly higher or lower, depending on the shape of the pony's underside, ensuring that each billet has equal pressure. In addition, should one buckle break mid-game, the other will hold, so the saddle will not slide off completely.

Fleece girth covers can be used on any type of girth to protect a pony from girth galls.

If at all possible, it is recommended that your girths be wiped down after every match. Pony sweat is full of salts and will dry out leather and rust metal very quickly.

The girth must hold the saddle securely in place, without causing the pony discomfort. A breastplate is often added, to prevent any chance of the saddle sliding backwards during the rigours of the game.

Over-girth

An over-girth is a thin, full girth, made of either leather or fabric, which wraps all the way around the pony and over the saddle. In the event that your girth does break mid-game, an over-girth will keep the saddle upright long enough for you to pull up your mount and change your equipment.

The over-girth fits over the top of the saddle. Note also the pad beneath the saddle.

Breastplate

Another crucial part of the polo pony's equipment is the breastplate; a thick leather strap that runs from one side of the saddle, around the front of the pony's chest and to the other side of the saddle. In a fast-moving, tough sport like polo, a breastplate is crucial to keep the saddle from sliding. See arrow in photo below.

A breastplate.

Leg protection for the pony

Polo wraps

The care of our ponies is a crucial part of our skill as polo players. Lameness is the number one cause of a pony missing a game. Horses and ponies carry the major part of their weight on their forelegs and it is in these limbs that most lameness occurs.

The staple polo wrap is what everyone uses when riding or playing. It is elasticated cotton or fleece with Velcro at the end to fasten

Polo wraps.

it. Contrary to popular belief, polo wraps do not actually prevent the fetlock joint from over-extending and thus preventing bowed tendons. The fetlock joint must bend and flex in unrestricted fashion, otherwise the joint would not be able to do what it's meant to do naturally. They do, however, provide protection from knocks and blows and damage caused by hooves (whether the pony's own, or another pony's) or by hard plastic outdoor balls.

Polo wraps must be put on correctly: if put on incorrectly, they can actually cause damage. Apart from the need to apply them with correct tension, one potential cause of damage can be if the Velcro fastenings are not in good order. If you have any concerns about this, reinforce them with electrical tape. The dangers of a foreleg polo wrap coming undone at a gallop are obvious. If a front wrap comes undone you risk the pony stepping on it with a hind foot and tripping himself. There's not a lot of things a pony can do to save himself from this sort of accident.

Wraps should be removed as soon as possible after play as they tend to get wet when ponies are sweaty, and will tighten when they dry, and can injure the tendons.

Boots

Protective boots such as tendon boots can be used on top of polo wraps for added protection. Not only will these provide added cushioning, they also guarantee that the polo wraps will not come undone mid-game.

Overreach boots, or bell boots, are a great investment. They are usually made out of rubber or a similar, durable material and are either closed or open in form. The closed boots are not easy to put on – they have to be stretched over the hooves – but, provided they are of the correct size, it is highly unlikely that they will come off during use. The other type can be opened up and fastened around the fetlock, with Velcro or some other form of fastening. They are thus much easier to fit than the closed boots, but the possibility exists of them coming undone.

These boots protect the pony's sensitive coronary band and heels from injury from their own, or another pony's, hooves. If the coronary band is injured badly enough, it can disrupt the growth of the hoof permanently.

Ready to play, wearing tendon boots over polo wraps, with bell boots protecting the coronary band and feet.

RIDER'S EQUIPMENT

Mallet

Mallets consist of three pieces: the grip, the cane and the head. The grip can be made to order depending on the player: women, children, men, large men, etc., and is wrapped in rubber to provide a secure hold and dry quickly when it gets sweaty. Attached to the end of the grip is the cloth sling, which wraps around the player's thumb, across the back of the hand and eventually rejoins the grip.

Most canes are made out of manau-cane, a thorny member of the palm family (not bamboo, as it is often assumed). Once cut, the cane is processed in several different steps to dry, straighten and preserve the material. You can also buy mallets made out of fibreglass and composite materials, designed to be more long-lasting. However, I find them cold and lacking the natural 'whip' that a wooden cane provides.

A 6–8 inch length of tipa hardwood is attached to the cane to form the head. The head can weigh anywhere from 160–240 grams (as in some

Mallets and boots in the polo barn.

other sports, weights and measurements in polo are a strange mixture of imperial and metric!). Several shapes and styles exist for the head: cigar-shaped, rounded, tapered, etc. Generally speaking, either the heel or both the toe and the heel of the mallet will be cut away at the bottom to allow the player to reach for poorly placed balls without getting caught up on the ground. A squat head lowers the centre of gravity of the head, adding loft to the ball. A taller head raises the centre of gravity.

The length, weight, flexibility (whippiness) and balance of a mallet can all be custom-ordered depending on the player's preferences. Women and children will generally prefer a lighter weight; players on larger mounts may want a longer mallet; some players, depending on the position they're playing, will want a very whippy or very stiff mallet. Whippy mallets tend to be more inaccurate and slow; they absorb a lot of the energy from the hand and snap back to natural with a slight delay. This makes it more difficult to perform quick follow-ups and corrections to the ball. All of these things must be taken into consideration when selecting a mallet. Some players will have a different length of mallet depending on the height of each pony they play, while others play with one length and adjust their swing accordingly.

A balanced cane is essential. The head and the cane should weigh about the same, making the fulcrum point three-quarters of the mallet towards the head. The closer the fulcrum is to the head, i.e. the heavier the head, the more driving power to your swing. However, heavy heads require stronger wrist movements and will naturally be slower. Shorter mallets can also drive well, if the cane weight decreases and the head weight remains the same. They are also quicker and easier to handle.

Clothing

Whites

The ancient polo players in Persia wore loose-fitting white clothes to counteract the heat. When the British cavalry learned polo, these clothes turned into white riding breeches (USA *britches*). Currently, most players simply wear white jeans or white breeches. Jeans, while more fashion-able at the after-polo parties, can cause rubbing owing to the seam on the inner leg. When playing for the first time at a new club, unless told otherwise, it is a sign of respect to wear white breeches or jeans.

Shirts

Back In 1913, the sport lent its name to a shirt, specifically developed by Brooks Brothers, for the playing of polo. The button-down collar was created in an attempt to keep the shirt's collar out of the player's face during a game. While traditionally the Brooks Brothers' polo shirt was the only option for polo players, today's players enjoy the benefits of many different styles and moisture-wicking materials. Obviously, in a formal game at any level, players will wear a team strip.

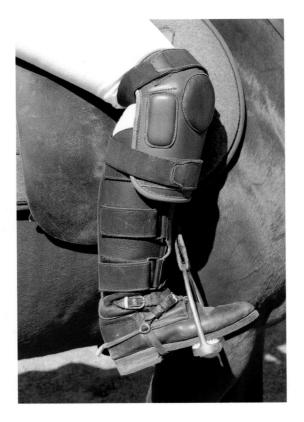

Boots

There are two basic styles with polo boots nowa-days: the cowboy boot and the traditional English polo boot. The traditional English boot can either have a single zipper up the front, or a zipper combined with Velcro straps. Both provide the same amount of protection, grip, function, etc. and the choice is a matter of fashion. I personally prefer the Velcro straps because, regardless of winter weight gain, even if the zipper does not zip all the way up, the Velcro ensures that the boots will fit. Clean and condition your boots after every ride. Your boots are probably the piece of leather closest to the sweaty pony and will receive the most abuse.

An English polo boot: the rider is also wearing kneepads and spurs.

When buying a new pair, make sure they are comfortable, but also keep in mind that over time the leather around the ankle will fold and bunch. Also use boot spacers, or a 1–1.5 litre bottle inside each boot to help boots keep their shape.

Protective equipment

Helmet

The most important piece of equipment in a player's tack box is the helmet – and wearing one in play is compulsory. It cannot be over-stressed how important it is to always wear a helmet when you're on horseback. One day I was training the mare La Loca, mentioned earlier. Although a notoriously difficult animal, who would throw herself on her back when pressured at all, we were going along nicely; she was calm, relaxed, focused. It had rained the day before and the ground was slippery underneath. As we cantered along, she hit a slippery spot with her inside hind leg and both of us went down. I wasn't wearing a helmet and walked away with severe concussion and bruised nerves. That was the only reminder I needed to always wear my helmet. Polo ponies can reach speeds of up to 40 miles an hour and a field ball can reach speeds of 110 mph. Like all sports, there are a number of uncontrollable variables that can be extremely dangerous and there is never a reason not to use a helmet.

As for other disciplines, there are various designs of helmet available that are suitable for polo, and consequent requirements/recommendations from the organising bodies. In 2012, the USPA passed a resolution requiring all players to wear helmets that have passed NOCSAE (National Operating Committee on Standards for Athletic Equipment) certification. In the UK, The Hurlingham Polo Association recommends following the British Horse Society recommendation for safety standards of helmets: 'hats which comply with PAS 015, BS EN 1384, EN 1384 (providing it has a CE mark), ASTM F1163 or Snell E2001, with either the Kitemark or SEI'. Since technological advances

THE COMPLETE GUIDE TO **POLO**

continue, it is possible that further new designs will become available and recommended in the future.

Glasses or faceguard

Most clubs have a rule that either sports glasses/goggles or a faceguard must be used when playing league games. Faceguards offer more coverage and protect the entire face from impact but they can be awkward, restrict movement of the head and can be found cumbersome. Sports glasses, on the other hand, offer no protection to the nose and mouth of a player, but are much more comfortable.

A USPA safety committee found that facial injuries comprise 19 per cent of all injuries suffered by polo players and are the second most common type of bodily injury; 65 per cent of the facial injuries occurred to players who did not wear facemasks.

Gloves

Gloves, obviously, protect the player's hands. Some players wear gloves on both hands; others wear one only, on either their mallet or their rein hand. You can buy polo gloves, but baseball batting gloves work just as well at half the cost.

Kneepads

Kneepads can be found in several styles and protect the rider's legs during a ride-off. They can be obtained with Velcro straps or buckles and are usually made of leather.

Baseball gloves work well for polo.

Aiding equipment

Whip

A dressage whip works well for polo. It needs to be long enough to wrap around your leg if you need to use it without taking your hand off the reins, but short enough not to get in the way. You should get accustomed to always playing with a whip, whether it is needed or not. It should be used as an aid to reinforce your leg aids; it should never be used as punishment. A pony running away from pain has turned off his rational brain and is running out of fear, which means he will run through a fence if necessary to get away from the pain. Plus, a player who makes a loud display of whipping their pony on the field is just showing ignorance and incompetence.

Spurs

Spurs are tools to aid in communication with your pony. When a pony is galloping, his body releases adrenalin, to help him in his flight/fight reflex. When a pony is in this mind-set, he's going to be less responsive to your aids than if he were calm and relaxed.

Close-up view of a spur. Spurs should always be fitted so that the ends are curved downward, not upward. The HPA specifies that spurs must not exceed 1¼ inches in length.

Spurs should only be used once you have a stable enough seat that your upper body and lower body can work independently of each other. A rider wearing spurs should be able to ride with their legs in a neutral position, and have the control to be able to apply the spurs only as needed. Also, the application of spurs should only be a back-up of the initial aids if a pony is unresponsive.

CHAPTER THREE

Horsemanship

THE IMPORTANCE OF your pony on the polo field cannot be underestimated. His athletic ability, training and your ability to manoeuvre him accurately will determine your value as a player. Most players you talk to, when asked, will readily tell you their ponies are 80–90 per cent of the game. In fact, a person's handicap can change by up to two goals, either way, based on their rapport with a particular pony and how well that pony is trained.

SELECTING POLO PONIES

The term 'pony', although widely used in the sport of polo is, in fact, something of a misnomer, as there are currently no height (or breed) restrictions to the animals in polo. Prior to 1899 the height limit for ponies was 13.2 hands measured at the withers (a 'hand' being 4 inches). In 1899 it was raised to 14.2 hands or 58 inches. In 1919 the height restrictions were abandoned.

When you start to learn polo, you will be riding a pony either borrowed or supplied by the person or organisation teaching you, and will be some distance away from being ready to select your own ponies. However, when the opportunity arises, ride and play on as many different ponies as possible; not only will this help you to become a better rider, it will also give you the chance to develop a feel for what size of pony you feel better on. I've seen all kinds: men over 6 feet tall on 14 hand Thoroughbreds, and women just over 5 feet on 16 hand giants. A good saying (albeit an exaggeration to make the point) is that you want an 18 hand mount that plays like a 14 hand one, the meaning being that a larger mount will have an obvious mass and height advantage over others in a ride-off – but bigger animals often stop and turn like 18-wheelers. The smaller ponies are generally handier and more agile, but are easily intimidated in ride-offs.

A lot of polo ponies are cutting or Argentine gaucho ponies. These breeds make great low- to medium-goal polo ponies, but most high-goal players are on Thoroughbreds or Thoroughbred crosses. Only animals with a good degree of Thoroughbred blood have the speed and stamina to gallop the long distances required in polo. High-end polo ponies are, in fact, bred specifically for polo, from successful playing stock. Polo requires not only a level of physical ability and strength, but also a certain 'heart' that can't be judged when analysing potential polo mounts. You need a pony who is brave, will attack a play, but still be obedient and willing, and breeding from proven stock increases the genetic probability of this 'heart' being inherited.

Getting a polo pony ready for a game.

While breeding specifically for polo is an excellent plan when the time and resources are available, it is also a risk. Unless you clone, you cannot affect the genes specifically to breed for the qualities you want. You can hope that the offspring has the best qualities of both sire and dam, but no equine is perfect, and imperfect qualities can be bred into offspring. Regardless of the genetics, you will have to wait at least five or six years to know whether the progeny will make a top-notch polo mount.

Prior to 2007 in the USA, many ex-racehorses, although excellent athletes, found their way to the slaughterhouses when their racing careers were over. In 2007 the last slaughterhouses in the USA that accepted horses were closed down. While this is excellent news for horse welfare, it also presented the problem of extra ex-racehorses with no place to go. In 2011 a law was passed allowing for the slaughter of horses again, but the market is still flooded with horses needing a home and a job.

Ex-racehorses offer an alternative source of polo mounts, and some can prove excellent in the role. They are already broken to the saddle and bridle, already know how to stand for the farrier, and load onto transport. Those who've shown aptitude on the racecourse are likely to have the heart needed to play and, with the Thoroughbred capacity for learning, they can become successful polo mounts after only a few months. Of course, they need to be taught to neck-rein, get used to the mallet and be desensitised to the prospect of being bumped, but all potential polo ponies need to learn these things. With many excellent horses out there, in need of a new job, it is advantageous to consider them as potential polo mounts.

FITNESS

Any given chukka is, in principle, 7½ minutes long, but the play clock stops when the ball goes out of bounds or the referee calls a foul. For this reason, a '7½-minute' chukka can often take up to half an hour.

In outdoor polo, a polo pony can run up to 3 miles in one chukka. In addition to galloping, a polo pony must make hard stops, roll-backs, lean into other ponies during a ride-off, and listen attentively to the rider's aids. Thus a polo pony must have the endurance of a racehorse, but the handiness of a cutting horse.

Because of the demands made upon them, polo ponies are substituted after every chukka although, in low-level polo, a pony can be played twice in one game, as long as he is given adequate time to rest between chukkas. Therefore a 'string' of ponies is needed, anywhere between four and six individuals, depending on the level of polo being played and, when at all possible, a player should maintain one or two 'spares'.

Attaining and retaining the fitness levels necessary is important, and the former is a process that cannot be rushed. At the beginning of the season, the ponies have usually had a couple months off. To begin getting them back into shape for the season, take them out for long walks for the first couple of weeks once or twice a day. Step them up to increasingly long periods of trotting once or twice a day for the next couple of weeks. Once they are comfortable with this work, take them out for periods of cantering once or twice a day for a week or so. (In the sport of polo, this work is usually done in 'sets' whereby you'll ride one pony whilst leading one or two more on either side, thus exercising five at a time.) After that, you can begin taking them out for canter work in the morning, and stick and balling (see Appendix), or playing slow practice chukkas in the afternoon.

The goal behind every session is to push them just hard enough so that they sweat and breathe a little heavier, without pushing them so hard as to cause distress or injury.

Once the season is in full swing, your maintenance exercise routine will depend on how many times a week you play. If you're playing three or more times a week, the only exercise I would recommend would be long periods of walking the morning before a game or on their days off to alleviate stiffness and keep them supple.

THE AIDS

When mounted, humans have certain tools at their disposal with which to communicate their wishes to their horse or pony. These are the 'aids'. We have our hands, legs, weight/seat and voice.

As an overall rule, it is always best to remember, when applying the aids, to use 'as little as possible, but as much as necessary'. To use stopping as an illustration, this means that if you wish to stop your pony, ask with as little pressure as possible, gradually increasing the pressure until your pony gives you the desired result. *Then release the pressure as soon as possible.* This release of pressure is a reward for the pony and teaches him exactly what you're asking for. The same principle applies for everything we do with our ponies.

Directional aids

There are two different forms of directional rein aids used in polo: direct and indirect reining. Direct reining means taking one rein, for example the right rein, and applying pressure on the right side of the pony's mouth until he turns to the right. Indirect reining, or 'neck-reining', is where the reins are held in one hand, and to turn to the right, for example, you take your hands across the pony's withers to the right, applying pressure on the left side of his neck. Direct reining is mainly used in training, or to reinforce the neck rein. Polo is played primarily with neck-reining, as your right hand holds the mallet. The reins and your whip are held in your left hand.

To assist neck-reining, the manes of polo ponies are clipped short. If the manes were left long, they could easily get tangled in fingers, reins and whips and this could be dangerous given the circumstances.

While the reins will direct the pony's forehand, your legs direct the pony's body. Your left leg, applied at the girth, or *slightly* behind it, on the left side of the pony, will push his body to the right. The converse holds true for your right leg. Your left leg, applied distinctly *behind* the girth, will push the pony's hind end to the right and vice versa. This is the aid the player applies when riding-off an opponent, to encourage the pony to move sideways, into the opposing pony.

Both legs, applied behind the girth, will signal for the pony to move; if the reins are slack, he will move forward; if his movement is restrained by the bit, he will move in reverse. A quick note on reverse (also called backing, or rein-back): it should never be used on the polo field. It is useful to teach the movement as a training exercise (see Rein-back, later this chapter), but this should only be done once the pony is obedient to the basic aids and well trained in going forward. If a 'hot' pony is taught how to reverse early on, he may use it as an escape mechanism during throw-ins. If the pony does not find release from something unpleasant (a group of others vying for position, a painful bit, etc.) by backing up, the next logical step for him is rearing, which is extremely dangerous, even for the most experienced rider.

Fine-tuning the rein aids

Most of the bits used in polo have two sets of reins, an upper rein and a lower rein. The upper rein is connected directly to the bit rings, hence directly to the pony's mouth. The lower rein is generally connected to a gag ring, or the bottom of a shank of a Pelham (it would also be the curb rein on a double bridle). With any type of bit, the lower rein uses the bit itself as a fulcrum point and applies pressure to the back of the pony's head, just behind the ears. This action also causes the bit to rise in the pony's mouth and has more of a 'halt' effect than the upper rein. (See Bit Selection in Chapter 2 for more information).

There are two accepted ways of holding your reins in polo. The 'English' style has your snaffle rein running over the top of your index finger, and your curb rein between your index and middle finger. In the 'Argentine' style, you hold both sets of reins as if you were holding an ice cream cone. The top left rein goes over your index finger. Below that is the top right rein, below that the right bottom rein and between your little and ring fingers is the bottom right rein. In both styles, your top direct rein should have very little slack in it, while the bottom rein should have two or three inches of slack. You want the top rein to engage first, followed by the bottom rein as reinforcement. Both methods work well and players have reached 10-goal status using both. Experiment to see which method feels better to you.

English style of holding the reins.

Argentine style of holding the reins.

Pony's and rider's centres
of gravity aligned.

Centres of gravity and the seat

Pony's centre of gravity

It will be useful to keep in mind the fact that, when we ride a pony in a
game of polo, we are asking him to do things that he would never do
on his own, naturally. In addition to this, we're asking him to do these
things with the added weight of a rider on his back, a weight that has its

own centre of gravity. The pony's centre of gravity is generally located near the girth, approximately where a normally seated rider's knee would be, but moves in rhythm with his gait. Naturally, a larger proportion of an equine's weight is towards his forehand, with a lesser proportion towards the rear. This is the reason why riders in all disciplines are concerned with asking their horses to collect, or bring more of their weight to the hind-end, which is not that easy and requires training. The natural weight distribution is also the reason why most of cases of lameness appear in the forelegs.

Rider's centre of gravity

The polo pony is a professional athlete. The manoeuvres we ask him to perform require years of training and dedication, and it takes a very special combination of mental and physical sharpness to make a good polo pony. As we train and play polo we must be mindful that we each have our own centre of gravity and that this can move independently. That is why we must work on our own sense of balance and understand how it affects the pony. (Women, naturally, have a lower centre of gravity than men, which is advantageous when it comes to horsemanship.)

A good polo pony will move to step underneath your centre of gravity when he becomes out of balance, to save you both from a fall. Now, if our centre of gravity is approximately underneath our belly button, imagine where it is when the player is reaching hard for a hook, or leaning into an opponent during a ride-off. A lot of players will lean well out of the saddle and lean into their opponent with their entire upper body. This leaves the pony trying to maintain his and your combined centre of gravities; reacting to your movements. If you maintain your balance over the centre of the saddle, while applying your opposite leg to the opponent, the pony is free to use his own strength against the opposing pony. A pony will put much more mass into another pony if he has been well trained and is doing it of his own accord than if he is merely following your off-balance weight.

Rider's seat

In the ideal polo seat, your heels will be flexed, your lower legs hanging loosely from the knees. The knee should be just behind the pony's shoulder; not out in front of you so much that you resemble sitting on a couch, but not directly underneath you as if you were standing either. Find a position that allows you to sit comfortably, but rise into a half-seat quickly. A lot of polo is played in a half-seat: standing slightly in the stirrups, gripping with your thighs and calves, seat well out of the saddle, but balanced. If you watch videos of polo, you'll notice that professionals are in this position most of the time. It is the most stable position from which to hit the ball. A galloping pony's back can move a a good deal but, in a half-standing position, your ankles, knees and hips absorb the movement, and allow your upper body to remain stable. If your upper body is stable then, given that the ground is stable (level), you can hit the ball regardless of what the pony is doing.

It takes a lot of practice to build the muscles that facilitate this position. Riding muscles are used only in riding, and so are underdeveloped in the average person. They can strain quickly, and once injured are very slow to heal, so always err on the side of caution when exercising these muscles. Begin at walk, and gradually work your way up to trot and canter. Spend as much mounted time as possible standing in this position. You may grab the martingale strap, or front of the saddle or handful of mane (if the pony has one), to help you while you're learning your balance.

Another useful exercise is to ride as often as possible without stirrups. Take your feet out of the stirrups, cross the stirrups over in front of the saddle, on the pony's neck, and ride for at least 15 minutes without them, maintaining your leg position as if it you still had the stirrups. Again, the moment you feel as if you're straining to maintain this position, take back your stirrups.

The correct mounted position begins with your heels. The fashion used to be to play polo with the feet 'fully home' (all the way through the stirrups), with the feet held flat. Nowadays, though, it has been proven much safer and more efficient to keep the stirrup irons on the balls of the feet, with your heels below your toes. There are a few reasons why this position has proved advantageous. The first, of course, is safety. If, as you are galloping along, your pony should trip, or flip over, you want your feet to slip loose from the stirrups backwards, and keeping your heels down will ensure this. With your feet all the way 'home' in the stir-rups, there is the chance that a foot will slip all the way through and the stirrup iron can then get wrapped around your ankle. If this happens and you have a fall, your pony could end up dragging you, which could be fatal.

Even if your pony does not go down, keeping your heels down is essential to a secure, balanced seat. If your pony should trip, or stop short, or even begin to buck, keeping your heels down will keep your weight back and down and keep you from becoming unseated. I remember one day vividly: I was taking sets, with two ponies on each side, and was cantering leisurely up and down hills. I was, honestly, half asleep and not paying much attention, when my mare tripped and went down on both front knees. My hunter training made certain my heels were down and luckily, in the next stride, she was up on all four legs and cantering off again. In those situations, only a balanced seat and low heels will keep you safely on the saddle.

TRAINING ISSUES

Collection

For a polo pony to perform difficult manoeuvres well he must be collected. When a pony is collected, he is balanced from front to back. This not only makes him more ready to perform the next move, but in the long term will also protect him from common injuries caused by rough starts and stops, unbalanced turns, and sprawling gaits.

A collected pony will bring his hind legs well underneath himself, his head and neck will be arched gracefully and his back will be raised.

This takes more effort on behalf of the pony, but you will be able to tell clearly a pony who moves in a collected way. The top of his neck will have smooth, rounded muscling: the underside of his neck, by contrast, will not be overdeveloped. More than likely there will not be a dip in his musculature right before the withers. His chest and hind-end will be well developed and his abdominal region should tuck up well, like that of a greyhound or racehorse. A pony who does not use himself correctly will have a skinny, under-developed neck, a loose belly, and

A polo pony in action, moving in collected fashion.

under-developed hind-end. This can always be improved upon with training and exercise and is not a permanent fault. Horses and ponies will, like most humans, be naturally lazy and do as little work as possible, and hence they will move in a way that is inefficient in terms of carrying a rider unless taught and trained how to move correctly. It's almost the same as the difference between a human ballerina and someone who only moves away from their computer to fetch a snack.

Canter leads

The walk and trot are both balanced bi-lateral gaits, in which both sides of the pony should be moving equally. The canter, on the other hand, is different. If you watch a cantering pony closely, you will see that one hind foot hits the ground first, followed by the other hind foot and its diagonally opposite forefoot together, and then the other forefoot (for example, left hind foot, then right hind foot and left forefoot together, then right forefoot). You will also notice that the forefoot that moves independently comes further forward than the forefoot that moves as a pair. This individually moving foot is the pony's 'lead' – in the example above, the pony is in 'right lead', but the whole sequence of footfall can also be reversed, in which case a pony would be in 'left lead'.

In polo, we often train the ponies to automatically pick up the right-side lead. Around 75 per cent of your swings in polo are going to be on the offside, or hitting off of the right side of the pony. Because, on the right lead, the right foreleg is leading and stretching out further, the shoulder flattens, and gives us a nice platform from which to swing the mallet. Going around a turn, ponies will naturally pick up the lead for the direction they are moving, i.e. right lead if they are turning right. This gives them more traction and control. This solid platform is exactly what you want if you're hitting offside forehanders. If you are going to hit a nearside shot or you anticipate a sharp turn to the left and have the time to prepare your pony by changing leads, do so.

To check which lead you are on, ask your pony to pick up canter (see below for how) and look down at his shoulders. If you are on the right lead, the right shoulder will come more forward than the left. The pony essentially holds his body in a curve, as if he were cantering on a circle. Many riders will soon learn the 'feel' of the leads and be able to tell without looking down.

To ask for a particular lead, collect your pony by squeezing the reins and applying your legs slightly. Collecting him will lighten his forehand and allow him to push off well. A lot of beginners will kick their pony forward until the trot is faster and faster and eventually the pony 'falls' into a canter. The resulting gait is strung out and uncoordinated and does not set the pony up for stopping or turning quickly. Once your pony is collected, it helps if you turn his nose slightly in the direction of the required lead (but note that this should be a subtle indication, not an overt pulling outwards or backwards of the inside rein). Apply your outside leg well behind the girth and ask the pony to step up with it: it is this outside hind leg that begins the stride. As far as the seat is concerned, the canter aid in polo is rather different from disciplines such as dressage, in that we use our weight leaning forward to encourage the canter, so if you are asking for canter from trot, you will raise yourself into a half-seat, to signal this and free the movement of the pony's back. If you are asking from walk, remain seated and ask with your hips as well. When applying the outside leg, move your hips forwards, as if the pony had picked up the canter and you are merely following his movement.

Flying changes of lead

Say you are cantering down the field, on the right lead, stick and balling (see Appendix). You hit a back shot (see Chapter 4) and need to turn to the left to go pick it up. How do you switch to the left lead? As for every good transition, collect your pony. Tip his nose to the inside of the new direction and apply your outside leg (behind the girth) and outside seat bone to the new direction. If you time this well and he is moving well enough forward, a trained pony should swap leads easily. If he does not, some training may be required. A lot of ponies will learn to switch automatically, but it takes time and training and a certain level of athletic ability. Be sure to ask when his hind legs are leaving the ground. If he has any weight on his hind legs, he cannot switch them to begin the next stride. You will know when his hind legs leave the ground by watching his head. A pony's head and neck are stretched out as his hind legs leave the ground, so be sure to ask for the change when your pony's neck is extended. It can, however, take practise to get the timing right, so assistance from an instructor on the ground can be helpful.

To teach your pony flying changes of lead, carve out a rounded figure of eight in your field. The diameter of the circular elements should start out fairly large (around 30 yards), but can be gradually reduced to less than half that as things progress. Pick up the canter in either direction around the figure. As you come to the centre of the '8', bring the pony back down to the trot, flex his body to the direction of the new circle, and ask for that lead. If he still has trouble understanding your aids, patiently bring him back down to a trot and ask again, and again, until he understands it. Once he does what you are asking – which, at this stage, is performing a simple change of lead – let him walk and rest. If he does it particularly well, you can dismount and take him back to the stable. This rest will be the biggest reward for a job well done, and the pony will remember it for next time.

If the pony attempts to switch leads but is off balance or does not have the correct coordination, he may switch in his forelegs but not his hind legs. It will briefly feel as though you are on top of an egg scrambler or a washing machine. Bring him back down to trot and ask for the correct lead again. Be patient in this work. All ponies, just like humans, are essentially one-sided and will find one lead easier than the other. Those who are very stiff on one side, and find picking up one of their leads particularly difficult, will require suppling exercises to overcome this problem.

Once the pony is comfortable and confident with simple lead changes, reduce the number of trot strides between the two canter leads until you can perform the change 'flying' – i.e. without any intervening strides of trot.

Turns

It is very important that a polo pony learns to turn quickly, in balance. The following exercises familiarise him with the aids for turning, and improve his suppleness and responsiveness.

Turn on the forehand

Walk your pony alongside an arena wall or fence, but a few feet away from it, and halt. (You can also do this out in a field, but a barrier a few feet to one side can help initially.) Engage the reins lightly to arrest forward movement (but not so strongly that there is an incentive for backward movement). Place your outside heel (the heel closest to the wall), significantly behind the girth and nudge rhythmically into your pony's side. Continue nudging until he begins to step his hind end in the direction you are nudging – i.e. away from the wall. As he does so, his forehand will turn a little in the direction of the wall, which is why you need a little space to accommodate this. He should not move forward or backward, only pivot around his forehand. Subtle rein aids should prevent any forward movement, and judicious use of your inside leg should help prevent any attempt at stepping backwards.

This exercise is difficult, and if your pony ignores your outside heel or does not understand what you are asking, reinforce your heel with taps of the whip in time with the heel. The moment your pony begins to move, or show that he understands, or is at least trying to do what you are asking, cease the nudging. This is the reward he is looking for.

This exercise should be performed in both directions and it is worth noting that ponies (particularly young/semi-trained ones) often find it much easier to do one way than the other. Where that happens, it is a good indicator of one-sidedness that requires further suppling work.

Turn on the hocks

This is a precursor to the turn on the haunches in motion (USA *roll-back*). At halt, lift up the reins and engage your pony's mouth. Lean your weight on the seat bone in the direction you want him to turn and, using your outside rein and outside leg only (slightly behind the girth), ask your pony to move sideways around his inside hind leg. Ideally, he will move his forelegs around the hind legs, crossing one over the other as he goes. This is a great preparatory exercise for turns in motion and to limber up his chest and foreleg muscles. It is a challenging move to perform and should not be overdone. Practise equally in both directions.

Rein-back

Once your pony is sufficiently well-trained, and there is no chance of him using the movement dangerously, the rein-back, or reverse, can actually be a great suppling exercise. It requires control, balance, and concentration. The rein-back should be a two-beat diagonal gait, meaning that the left fore and right hind legs will move simultaneously as one beat, and the right fore and left hind move together in the second beat. When a pony decelerates during a game, he should do so with his head down, and his hind legs tucked well up underneath his body. His back will raise and his top-line will bow up and, if he is really balanced, he will dig his heels into the turf and give you a sliding stop. Some ponies, as the season goes on, or if they are out of condition, will be slow to stop. They will stop and turn like an 18-wheeler. To correct this, it is often advantageous to bring your pony down to a stop from a canter and ask him to back two or three steps. Doing this repeatedly without warning will get your pony thinking 'back' when you touch the reins.

To introduce the movement, come to a straight halt, retain even pressure on the reins, and nudge his sides gently with your heels. Your leg aids are asking him to move, but your hands are telling him 'not forwards'. If this is new to him, he may try to walk forwards, or toss his head, or even offer a turn on the forehand. Use your hands to prevent him from moving forward (but not to the extent of trying to drag him backwards, which will prove counterproductive), and keep asking until he gives you a step backwards. At the beginning, reward any hint of the idea of moving backwards. Progressively, you will ask him for one step, then two, then more. This exercise should help him learn to shift his weight backwards, and bring his hind legs underneath him.

See the Appendix for more mounted exercises to help you improve your horsemanship.

CHAPTER FOUR

The Swing

Ninety per cent of your polo is made up of four basic swings:

1. Offside fore

2. Nearside fore

3. Offside back

4. Nearside back

Other, not so common swings are:

1. Offside neck shot

2. Nearside neck shot

3. Under the belly (King's shot)

These less common shots are worth learning and practising once you have established the basics. A professional can help with the swing – see Wooden Horse in the Appendix.

One of the less common
shots – a neck shot.

SWING PRINCIPLES

While the direction of the swings, the angle of the mallet head, the set-up
and follow-through will differ for each swing depending on what you
want to accomplish, there are some very basic ideas that carry through
all of your swings.

Keep your eye on the ball

In almost every ball sport, keeping your eye on the ball is the first thing
you're taught. It's amazing how easy it is to blink at the moment of
contact between the ball and the mallet head, or lift your eyes to see
where the ball is *going to go*. I distinctly remember watching Roger

Federer one evening with an avid tennis player. He commented on Roger's head, and how his eyes, and therefore his head, remained fixed on the spot where the racquet struck the ball, even well through the follow-through of his swing. It makes perfect sense. Your eyes will tell your brain how far away your hand is from the ball. (You might think that the crucial point is how far the mallet head is from the ball, but the brain computes things in terms of where your body parts are.) If your head is moving, and therefore your eyes are moving, it will be much more difficult for you to gauge where the ball will be at the moment of impact. If your head moves in the act of your swing, it will be nearly impossible to adjust your hand and mallet to correct accordingly.

We can often get into the habit of lifting our head at the moment of impact, or just before, in anticipation of hitting the ball and wishing to follow it with our eyes for the next play. If you find yourself topping the ball often, this is the most probable cause. Practise stick and balling while actively leaving your eyes (and therefore your head) where the ball was at the moment of impact with the mallet, even after you've hit it. Your head will remain still and become a stable anchor for your shoulder and swing.

Keep your head over the ball

In the same spirit as the previous point, getting your head poised out over the ball will give your eyes and your hand a solid point of reference from which to gauge the distance of the ball. At the moment of impact with the ball, there should be a straight line between your head, hand and the ball. If your head is out directly over the ball, this will guarantee a straight shot.

Always start in two-point

If you look back at the black and white photos of polo from the beginning of the twentieth century, the riders' stirrup leathers are long, their legs are almost straight and they clearly swung from a seated position.

Over the generations, a style using shorter stirrup leathers developed, when riders realised that the more freedom they gave their mounts' backs, the better they performed. The two-point position was first developed in other disciplines to allow the horse's back the freedom of movement, and to provide a stable foundation for the rider over obstacles. It is the perfect combination between stability for the rider and freedom for the horse.

In the two-point position, the rider's ankles, knees and hips are flexed, while the crotch and backside remain poised just above the saddle. The joints act as shock-absorbers of the movement beneath the rider, allowing the rider's upper body to remain stable and still. If

A lofted offside forehand shot. In order to hit the ball accurately at speed, you need to develop a sound swing technique.

you watch videos of the great polo players, you will see that, while their ponies are galloping flat out, the players remain almost motionless. Using this position, regardless of what the pony does (changing leads, tripping, bumping, bucking) you will have a stable foundation from which to hit the ball.

Follow-through

The follow-through is crucial in all ball sports. During the wind-up of the swing, you want to get the head of the mallet as far forward as possible. The velocity, torque and power of the swing are dictated by how far the head of the mallet has to travel around the axis (your shoulder). If your swing is correct, the motion will start with your core, your hips and your shoulder. Stopping all of these moving parts at the moment of impact with the ball would leave a lot of momentum wasted.

Controlling the follow-through will also lend accuracy to your swing. To ensure you strike the ball with the most speed and accuracy possible, you should plan and control your follow-through to prevent any hesitation or changes in the angle of the mallet head.

OFFSIDE FORE SHOT – STAGES OF THE SWING

1. Wind-up

The natural position your hand is in while you are riding to the ball should be somewhere in front of your shoulder, closer to your right ear. To begin the swing, stand up in the two-point position (if you're not already there). In a single, fluid motion, twist through your hips and core in the saddle to bring your left shoulder parallel to the pony, or pointing at the ball, and your right hand back behind you, being careful not to throw the head of the mallet around your back to the nearside of the pony. There is a misconception that the higher your hand is, the

The top of the swing for an offside fore shot, just before the drop.

more power your swing will have. In fact, it is the distance of travel of the mallet head, rather than the plane of the swing, that is the contributing factor in the power generated. See photo opposite.

2. The drop

The power behind the swing obviously affects the distance that the ball will travel. A lot of riders confuse this, though, with the idea that they need to force the mallet swing with overt muscular effort. In fact, a swing that is forced is often a lot less effective than an apparently slower, more fluid, swing. The force behind the head of the mallet is directly related to the amount of inertia it picks up throughout the swing. This

The wind-up.

inertia is what's transferred to the ball to create forward motion. The inertia is created by the drop of the mallet from the wind-up position. If you watch high-level players, true masters of the sport, you'll notice how effortlessly and almost slowly they appear to swing.

The downward motion of the swing should start with your shoulder, move through the elbow (which should remain as straight as possible) and down through the wrist. The wrist will start in a bent position in the wind-up stance but, as the mallet comes down, the wrist should straighten out in one fluid motion, creating almost a flicking motion as the head of the mallet contacts the ball. The movement should be as fluid, relaxed and as controlled as possible. To perfect this, breathe in during the wind-up and out during the drop.

The drop.

3. Contact

The moment of impact with the ball is crucial. The sweet spot on the ball is just below its centre of gravity, or just below the mid-point of the ball. Lofting the ball, even a little, will increase its travelling distance because of the lack of friction it would encounter rolling along the ground. Ideally, a spectator should be able to draw a straight line from your head, over your elbow and wrist, and straight down to the ball. If your arm is a pendulum, it is crucially important that it is straight at the moment of contact. Some recommend holding the mallet loosely in your hand

Contact.

throughout the first half of the swing, and just squeezing your hand shut at the moment of contact with the ball. This, combined with the whippiness of the mallet, increases the speed of the mallet head.

4. Follow-through

As mentioned earlier, the follow-through is probably the single biggest game-changer between a player who merely hits the ball down the field and one who can place it strategically where intended. The speed that the mallet picks up during the first half of the swing will carry momentum with it, which will be your follow-through. If your swing stops right after contact with the ball, it was losing momentum the entire time, and the ball will not travel as far as it should. Always keep in mind your follow-through and you will guide the ball further and more accurately than if you don't. During the follow-through, your head should

The follow-through.

remain still and in place, but your eyes must follow the direction of the cane through the follow-through. If you move your head at all during the contact or the beginning of the follow-through it will throw off the entire swing.

NEARSIDE FORE SHOT – STAGES OF THE SWING

1. Wind-up

To begin the nearside fore shot, stand up in the two-point position and rotate your hips and your shoulders as far to the left as possible. Many players find that, by digging their right knees and swinging their right foot out away from the pony, they're able to twist further while giving themselves a balancing weight. I tend to straighten my left leg, stand up on it and rotate the rest of my body around it. Bring your mallet hand across your chest and as close to your left shoulder as possible, while maintaining contact on the reins. Be sure not to pull your rein hand to the left as you turn because your pony will end up moving left and running over top of the ball.

2. The drop

The nearside fore shot is actually hit with the back of the mallet head. Many beginners will try to rotate their hands to hit it on the front of the mallet (where they would hit the offside fore shot), but they soon find out that their follow-through is impossible. Again, to maximise the distance the mallet head has to travel, and hence to give you more strength to your swing, straighten your arm as soon as possible during the drop. Throughout the drop, you will keep your head over the ball, maintain eye contact, and twist with your navel and shoulders. You won't be able to utilise your hips so much as you would in the offside fore shot because your follow-through will still be on the left side of the pony.

A player winding up to take a nearside fore shot.

3. Contact

The principles of the contact for the offside fore shot apply to the nearside fore shot as well. You want a straight line, perpendicular to the ground, to be drawn from your shoulder, hand, and ball at the moment of contact. Again, you want to strike the ball when it is in line with your pony's forefeet.

4. Follow-through

If you have done your preparation for this shot, got as far out of the saddle as possible and twisted to the left sufficiently, your mallet head will end up to the left of your pony's head. If you have not twisted enough, you will end up slicing your swing underneath the his head. This shot takes particular practice because many beginners find it difficult to maintain control of their reins while twisting enough to hit the ball accurately. Also, hitting the ball with the back of your mallet will feel unnatural at the beginning, and the distance to the ball will be different than on the offside forehand because of how much you are twisting.

OFFSIDE BACK SHOT/TAIL SHOT – STAGES OF THE SWING

1. Wind-up

Most beginners try to perform the back shot from a seated position. While this is possible, it will severely limit your ability to aim the shot and control the follow-through. Begin the swing in your two-point position, with your mallet hand beside your face/shoulder. Again, you will want to lean over the right side of your pony to get your head above the ball, but you will not need to lean as far forward. You will hit the ball when it passes just under your foot, so you will want to be up in two-point, but not perched out forward.

2. The drop

You will, again, stretch your arm out forward as far as possible, with the back of your hand facing forward and down. While keeping your head still, allow the weight of the mallet to drop. There are two kinds of back shots that are preferable in polo: open and closed. A back shot hit in a straight line directly behind you will usually end up hitting a player behind you, and potentially going into the hands of your opponent. For an open back shot, you will rotate the mallet head slightly open, which will cause the ball to travel at an open angle away from you. With a closed back shot, you have more room to begin your swing further out from the line of the ball. When extending your mallet hand forward, bring it out to the right about a foot. This will help the angle of the shot. You can't bring it out too far because the follow-through will end up hitting the pony's legs, but a foot or so out and you should still be able to clear them. In addition to this, you will turn the mallet head in, which will cause the ball to travel just behind your mount's legs.

3. Contact

The player on the right has just struck an offside back shot.

You want to make contact with the ball as it passes just under your foot. Again, you want to make sure a straight line is formed by your shoulder, hand, and mallet head. Depending on which angle you've hit the ball, your mallet head will either be pointing away from you or in towards you.

4. Follow-through

With the open back shot, you won't be able to follow-through in the direction of the ball, because the beginning of the swing will have been parallel to your pony. While you'll rely on the angle of the mallet head to give your ball the direction you need, the follow-through is still important as it was ensure that you do not slow down or hesitate before contacting the ball, and will thus ensure you get distance from your shot. With the closed back shot, you will be able to carry your follow-through behind the pony's hind legs.

NEARSIDE BACK SHOT/TAIL SHOT – STAGES OF THE SWING

1. Wind-up

As with the nearside fore shot you will want to stand up in the stirrups as tall as possible and rotate your hips and shoulders to be as parallel with the pony as possible. Instead of beginning with your mallet to the left of your head, you will begin with it on the right. Many beginners find that anchoring their rein hand onto the pony's neck or withers helps them avoid accidently directing their mount over the ball.

2. The drop

Begin the drop by stretching your mallet hand as far forward, left of the pony's head, as possible. This will ensure that your mallet travels the largest oval possible. Your drop will begin with your abdominals, and flow up through your shoulder, wrist, and eventually mallet head. Unlike the nearside fore shot, you will hit the ball with the front of the mallet head, as opposed to the back. Because of this, this shot is more natural feeling than the nearside fore shot.

The top of the swing for a nearside back shot.

3. Contact

As with the offside back shot, you have two options for the angle of the nearside back shot: open and closed. An open shot, again, will send the ball away from you and the line of the ball. A closed back shot will send the ball behind your mount. Again, the same rules apply: create a straight line between your shoulder, hand and mallet head at the moment of contact.

4. Follow-through

As with the offside back hander you'll be able to follow through on the closed back shot (across the tail) as opposed to the open back shot.

Follow-through on the nearside back shot is particularly difficult because you'll be crossing in front of your own body, so getting up out of the saddle and twisting is even more important. Ensuring you are twisted to the left as much as possible will help give you the freedom of movement you will need for your follow-through.

CHAPTER FIVE

Game Play and Strategy

GAME BASICS

Each polo match consists of four to six periods, called chukkas. In both the field and the arena forms of the game, each chukka lasts 7½ minutes. Generally, the bell will sound once at the 7-minute mark, and then twice at 7½ minutes to signal the end of the chukka. If a team scores, the ball hits the sideboards (in outdoor polo) or is knocked out of bounds, the chukka stops immediately. Other than that, play is continuous and only stops if the whistle is blown for a foul, or if a rider or pony is severely injured. If a penalty occurs after the 7-minute mark, time will be allowed to take the penalty, which will usually end in the termination of the chukka. At the end of each chukka, players will be allowed adequate time (nominally 4 minutes) to change their mounts. Generally speaking, players will change their mounts as quickly as possible, but will enjoy a longer break during half-time.

Outdoor polo is played on a grass field, 300 yards in length by 160 yards in width. Generally, short wooden boards are set up along the perimeter to help keep the ball in play. A generous 'out of bounds' area

Relaxing before the game.

should exist and players who are technically out of bounds can still make a play at the ball. There are four players to a team in outdoor polo, and during half-time, it's traditional for spectators to walk out onto the field and help replace the 'divots' created by the ponies' hooves. Outdoor polo balls are a hard plastic, 3–3½ inches in diameter and 3½–4½ ounces in weight. In outdoor polo, after each goal is scored, the teams switch sides and defend the opposite goal.

Arena (indoor) polo will be in an enclosed area 300 feet in length by 160 feet in width. Usually there will be netting up along the goal-posts to help keep the ball in play. If the ball is hit from the far side of the halfway line and scores a goal either directly, or by bouncing off the wall without being touched by any mount or another player, it will be two points. The arena ball must be no less than 12½ inches or more than 15 inches in circumference (which approximates to 4–4¾ inches in diameter) and weigh 170–182 grams. In arena polo, teams switch sides at the beginning of every chukka, not after every goal.

In a game as fast and furious as polo, it is important to understand the underlying principles and strategies.

Every player who is registered with their country's governing body is granted a handicap based on their skill, knowledge of rules and game-play, and their horsemanship. Handicaps range from -2 to 10, with -2 being the complete beginner, and 10 being the absolute best in the sport.

PRINCIPLES OF DEFENCE AND OFFENCE

Defence

There are two major defensive plays in polo: hooking and riding-off (also known as bumping.) Which you decide to do will depend on your location relative to your opponent, and where your opponent has the ball.

Hooking

If your opponent has the ball on the side of the pony that you are on, your best bet will be to go for a hook. Hooking, blatantly defined, is hitting your opponent's mallet with your own to prevent your opponent connecting successfully with the ball. Often this means you will both miss a play on the ball and ride on, leaving the ball for teammates behind you.

Most beginners will try to hook by merely keeping their mallet down and hoping their opponent's swing gets interrupted. If you do this an experienced opponent will swing hard through the 'hook', knock your mallet out of the way and play the ball, or dribble the ball around out of the your reach. The better hook is actually a downward swing, not necessarily for the ball, but just enough to give your mallet the momentum to really knock your opponent's mallet out of position. If you do have a play for the ball, either forward or backwards, take it. It's much better to take possession of the ball and make a play than merely upset your opponent's play.

Keep in mind, though, that if you hit the ball backwards and don't have any teammates to pick it up, you'll merely be passing it from one opponent to another. The better decision in this instance would be to try to take the ball forward, in your possession, and turn to set up for the next play.

Riding-off (Bumping)

The second defensive option a player has at their disposal is the ride-off or bump. It is exactly how it sounds. When your opponent has the ball, and you are not in a position to hook them, or do not want to hook and leave the ball behind you, bumping, or riding your opponent off the line of the ball is the obvious choice. To perform this manoeuvre successfully, you must not cross the line of the ball, or impede the right of way. Often your opponent may fall back in an attempt to draw you in front of them for the foul. Practising the 'tag' exercise in the Appendix will help you anticipate this move.

To give your pony the advantage of mass, make contact with your opponent only when your knee is in front of your opponent's on the saddle. This will ensure that your pony's shoulder is in front of your opponent's mount's shoulder, giving yours the advantage. Be careful to keep your contact elbow to your side. Often, especially when riding-off an opponent on our left side, we will pull the reins hard left, across our opponent's mount. This can be interpreted as 'throwing an elbow' and can result in being dismissed without the opportunity for the team to substitute.

Another controversy you will hear about a lot is whether or not to lean into the ride-off. Some players will lean into their opponent, thinking that their added mass will help win the ride-off. Other players remain perfectly balanced, knowing that while the transfer of their additional weight will certainly knock their own mount off balance, it will not have an overall effect on the bump, when compared to the two mounts. Some players will wait to the very last moment before contact, then stand in their stirrups and throw their weight violently into their opponent. Their mount, in an attempt to stay balanced and remain upright, will make a drastic shift towards the opposing pony. Personally, I would much rather *train* my pony to ride-off another, than rely on unbalancing my pony in order to win.

Offence

While, generally speaking, playing your position and marking your opponent will ensure you're in the proper position on the field, there are a few offensive guidelines to keep in mind.

'Man, line, ball'

The first and most important rule in polo is 'man, line, ball'. The purpose behind this axiom is to direct the novice player where to focus. It is natural and easy for a player to fall into the trap of focusing only on the ball. 'Man, line, ball' encourages a player to focus on just that: the opponent, the line, and then the ball, in that order.

Triangle formation

As a basic rule, when you find yourself in possession of the ball and are making a move towards your opponents' goal, it is good practice to hit towards the boards when at the middle of the field, and more directly towards the goal the closer you get to it. This draws a triangle on the field, with the widest part at the midfield mark, and the points at either goal-mouth. This practice prevents an opponent from stealing the ball and making an easy move on your goal. See diagram overleaf.

Backing-up your teammates

If ever you find yourself behind a teammate who has the ball, you should position yourself to be behind them to back them up, in case they should miss. The player who misses the ball, should then either move up and reposition for a pass, or move out of the way of teammates coming up from behind, and drop back to be able to back up the second player.

PLAYING POSITIONS

In the following explanation of playing positions, to help make things doubly clear, the position numbers of 'opponents' are set in bold.

Playing the No. 1 position

Playing No. 1 requires the greatest amount of discipline and diligence of all the positions, yet it's where most of us get started. The reasoning behind starting a new person in the No. 1 position is that there will be three other teammates backing up should this player miss the ball. The

Triangle
formation.

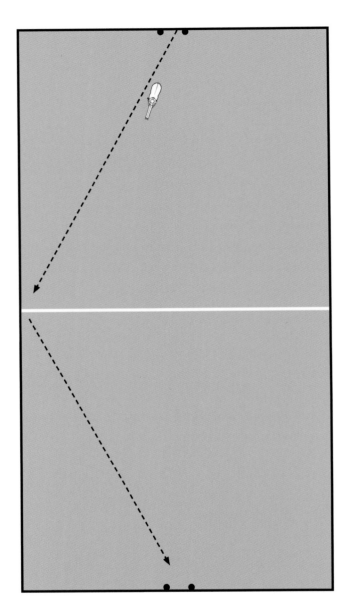

disadvantage of this is that the No. 1 is left defending against the **No. 4**
of the opposite team, who is usually the most experienced player.

While this can be frustrating at first, the best thing to concentrate on
is marking the opposing **No. 4** as closely as possible. It ancient polo, the
No. 1 didn't even have a mallet and, to this day, a good practice that some
coaches use is to make a player play a chukka without a mallet. The idea

here is that defence is the best offence: if you can neutralise the most experienced player on the opposite team, you are, in essence, earning the number of goals for your team equal to that player's handicap. For example, if a 0-goal No. 1 is able to take a 4-goal **No. 4** completely out of the game defensively, the No. 1 has effectively gained those 4 goals on their team's handicap. In practice, the opposing **No. 4** will usually have considerable experience and will be able to anticipate the play and will never be far out of position. However, while it's not always possible to neutralise a much higher-handicapped player, the practice will improve your horsemanship and anticipation immensely.

When your team is on the defence, you as No. 1 must remain back, never being so far away from the opposing **No. 4** that you risk getting caught off guard when he suddenly gets the ball, but far enough away that, should one of your teammates manage to back the ball, you will be able to jump on it and take it towards goal. If you do get caught out of position, you have generally left the best player on the opposite team free to make the play he wants, and you have effectively made the game three against four.

The second job of the No. 1 is offence. On the offence, you should be far enough forward that, should the ball come up to you, you'll have a good run at goal. Conversely, do not be so far forward that you are out of reach of your No. 2's swing. You should always be between your No. 2 and the goal, and ideally with the opposing **No. 4** on your nearside. With the opponent on your nearside, the only play he will have will be to bump you, but if you've prepared for this, you will give yourself enough space to be bumped.

Many times, the No. 1 and No. 2 will be closely handicapped and will often interchange positions. If your No. 2 has the ball, but you're guarded too close by the opposing **No. 4**, or your No. 2 is wide open, your best play here is to block the opposing **No. 4** and let your No. 2 take the ball to goal. As a general rule, if you are closely guarded, but receive the ball, it is always better to leave it rather than swinging wildly and perhaps moving the ball far enough so that your No. 2 will not have a play on it.

All players should learn to play the No. 1 position. Devereux Milburn (10-goal USA), a great back, called a No. 1 'the greatest asset a team can have'. It requires discipline, an understanding of team dynamics, excellent riding skills, and extreme flexibility. A few exercises to use to improve your ability as No. 1 are:

1. Throughout the chukka, try to visualise where you should be on offence and on defence.

2. Practise taking half swings on goal from many different angles. The opportunity for the No. 1 to shine and make goals will usually be closely guarded and half swings will be your most effective move.

3. Take time dribbling, and manoeuvring the ball in and out of obstacles.

4. Practise turning the ball from the corners of the field and taking it to goal.

5. Without mallets, play tag on horseback with a teammate (see Appendix). This will hone your skills in anticipating the movement of an opponent and help you guard better.

Playing the No. 2 position

As No. 2 you will have many of the same responsibilities as the No. 1, but the emphasis will be a lot less on scoring and more on feeding the ball up to your No. 1, if he is open. As No. 2 you will have to be well mounted because this position requires chasing down balls and guarding the opposing **No. 3.**

Offence

On offence, with the ball, the No. 2 will be either looking to pass it up to No. 1, or will call to No. 1 to 'take the man' and will take the ball on towards the goal. The No. 2 will have the most opportunity to take risks offensively. In contrast to the No. 3, who will have back-up from just one teammate, the No. 2 will have back-up available from two.

Defence

On defence, depending on where their own No. 3 is, No. 2 will often switch back and forth between guarding the opposing **No. 2** and **No. 3**. Just as with No. 1, if No. 2 can effectively disarm the opposing **No. 3**, who will generally be higher handicapped, this play will effectively gain the opposing **No. 3**'s number of goals for the team.

Attributes

In addition to switching places fluidly with No. 3, No. 2 should also be able to switch positions with No. 1.

In addition to being well mounted, as mentioned, No. 2 should have the courage to really push the opposing **No. 3**, and have excellent mallet work. In order to play this position well, you should practise making shots at difficult angles, dribbling, and should be able to hit the long ball consistently. The longer you can hit consistently, the further up the No. 1 can be for a pass, stretching out the offensive play.

The biggest mistake you have to guard against committing as No. 2 is being suckered out of position. It can be easy for No. 2 to get caught up in playing defence. If you do, you will miss a well-placed backhander by your No. 3 or No. 4, allowing the opposition to pick up the ball.

Some exercises to help improve your No. 2 play

1. Throughout the chukka, mentally keep track of your No. 1 and No. 3. You should be able to know their position on the field without having to look for them.

2. Take time dribbling.

3. Play keep-away with a friend.

4. Practise turning the ball from the corners of the field and taking it to goal.

Playing the No. 3 position

Depending on your team's strategy, No. 3 can often be the best player on the team. The No. 3 is the revolving door between defence and offence; the pivot point of the entire team. The responsibility of No. 3 is turning every ball into an attack for his team, and this requires the ability to switch from defence to offence seamlessly. The No. 3 must have excellent field awareness and must be able to think two or three plays ahead.

Offence

While No. 1 and No. 2 often take the most glory on offence, it is No. 3's responsibility to fight for possession of the ball and feed it forward to their No. 1 or No. 2, thus turning it into offensive play. To play this position you must therefore master the long ball. Simply hitting long shots is not enough; you must be able to hit them consistently, with accuracy. A long shot, poorly placed, is just a turnover to the opposing team.

Defence

Notwithstanding the offensive role, No. 3's most important role is in defence. As No. 3, you must not get caught up in the rush for the ball, or ball-hogging, or get caught out of position. Like a midfielder in soccer, as No. 3 you must hang back, always being between the opposing team and the goal you are defending. Ideally, you will be able to antici-pate several plays in advance and be able to win possession of the ball and either turn the play, or foil your opponents enough to prevent a goal.

Another requirement of No. 3 is mastery of the penalty shot from all angles, which includes the ability to loft the ball at will. Penalty shots often make up a sizable portion of the final score, so having a player who will consistently land the penalty shots is essential to a team.

In summary, the No. 3 role requires excellent hand-eye coordination, mallet control, field vision and anticipation – in short, and ideally, mastery of the sport. Therefore the No. 3 will often be the most experienced, most talented player on the team and a lot can be learned from watching a talented No. 3 in any game.

Playing the No. 4 position

There are no goalies in polo, and the primary responsibility for No. 4 is defence. Generally speaking, he will remain between the halfway mark and the goal he's defending, and will take up a position between the opposing player with the ball and the goal. It's also No. 4's job to make sure the ball stays at the opposite end as much as possible.

Polo is, generally speaking, an attacking game. There are only two defensive plays and neither one is as easy as any attacking move.

A team's No. 4 should be the player with the best vision of the entire field, the best ability to anticipate plays and the one with the longest hit. In a way similar to a No. 1, strategy and proper positioning are essential in a No. 4, who should also be handy enough with the mallet to be able to wrestle the ball away from an opponent and place it within a teammate's reach.

Once No. 4 has retaken possession of a ball, all three teammates should be turning and positioning themselves for a pass upfield. Turning the ball is always a better option than simply backing it. If you back a ball, you may not give your teammates enough time to position themselves properly, and you'll be shooting the ball into a field containing three teammates and four opponents. If the opposing **No. 1** is guarding you too tightly to allow for turning the ball, a back shot that places the ball on the offside of your teammate (already turned and waiting for it) will be just as advantageous.

A strong No. 4 will allow his No. 3 to play a more offensive role, strengthening a team's attack. While as No. 4 you will generally stay in the half of the field you are defending, you must always keep track of your opposing **No. 1**. If the **No. 1** is sufficiently skilful, you may have to be more active in seeking to neutralise this opponent.

During a line-up, as No. 4 you should maintain a couple of pony-lengths between yourself and your No. 3. You should be in a position to collect a stray ball if it should escape the other players and come out the back. If the ball should pass you, you'll be forced to turn to chase it. You should also be able to anticipate the new line of the ball and adjust appropriately.

CHAPTER SIX

Rules

WITH THANKS TO THE USPA and HPA for their permission, I have in this chapter broken down the key rules for the outdoor game as covered in both handbooks. I highly recommend reading and devoting time to studying the USPA or HPA rulebooks themselves. While the majority of the rules of both bodies are the same, I have noted instances in which there is some difference.

TEAM MAKE-UP

In an outdoor polo match, there will be four players to a team, where one of the players is nominated as the captain. The captain is the only member of the team who can speak to officials on behalf of the team. The only time a player other than the captain may appeal for a time out, is in the instance of tack malfunction or if he is concerned for the safety of his mount. This is mainly to avoid players 'working the umpire'. Even something as seemingly benign as thanking the umpire for a call in your favour can be taken as 'working the umpire'. Often, polo players will raise their mallets in an appeal for a call in their favour, but technically this can result in a penalty.

To qualify for a tournament, the total handicap of a team must fall within the limits of the event. It is possible that, during the course of a tournament, the officials will decide that a player is either under- or over-rated and will change a player's handicap between games. If this happens, and pushes a team over or under the limits of the tournament, the team will be allowed to finish the tournament at the new rating.

In a USPA regulated tournament, if this change in handicap pushes a team 2 goals over, or under the limits, the team will *not* be allowed to continue and substitutions will have to be made to conform to the limits of the tournament.

In a HPA regulated tournament, a high-goal team (any over 22 goals) will be allowed to play at the new handicap, regardless of how many goals over the tournament limits it is. Any team below 22 goals will only be allowed to play 1 goal over tournament limits.

If a player must be substituted, the handicap of the substitute must allow the team to adhere to the rules above.

The HPA rule book has an additional caveat, stating that if any player, whose handicap was raised during mid-season, pushes his team's aggregate handicap over the tournament limits, *and* must be substituted during a match, the substitution must be based on the initial handicap of the player. Ideally, this will bring the team back down to the tournament limit. However, if a second player on that team must be substituted, the initial total handicap of the team may stand.

During a regulated tournament, the schedule is agreed upon in advance by the host club tournament committee. If one or more of the players on a team is/are not mounted and ready to play at the start time of their match, the team may play without them as long as their total handicap remains within the limits of the tournament. If it does not, or if the players are severely late, the umpires will declare it a forfeit. A player who is, for example, stuck in traffic and certain to be late, may call the committee and ask for a delay in the start time of the match. Once the start time arrives, the decision is up to the umpire.

The USPA and the HPA differ on their requirements for sponsors and/or registered player members.

In every USPA registered tournament, each team shall have at least one sponsor (a primary and secondary if there are more than one), and have a minimum of one registered player member in addition to the sponsor.

The HPA rule book does not state a requirement for the number of sponsors and/or registered player members.

Players

The USPA and the HPA have varying rules regarding substitutions. However, all players must have paid their registration fee and have a current handicap to be allowed to play.

In the USPA, no player is allowed to play for more than one team during a tournament unless their usual team has already been disqualified from the competition and that individual player is then used as a substitute.

In the HPA, the tournament committee may agree to a substitute player who has, or will, play for another team. However, a player whose team is already disqualified will take preference.

There is also a difference between the USPA and HPA in how a player may proceed if his eligibility is in question:

In a USPA tournament, a player will be allowed to play while the tournament committee researches his eligibility. If it is determined that the player is not eligible, the game will be considered a forfeit by the offending team.

In a HPA tournament, no player is allowed to play if the tournament committee is not able to verify the player's eligibility.

There are several limitations the USPA has enacted, in order to promote safety, which may make a player ineligible to play in a USPA tournament:

- any player with a -2 or 'N' (Novice) handicap;
- a player with a handicap of -1 may not play in an 8+ goal game;
- each team can have no more than one -1 goal player in any event of 4+ goals;
- at no point may the handicap of an individual player be greater than the upper limit of the event;
- in any USPA tournament, where the upper handicap limit is 4+ goals, the handicap of any individual player must not exceed ¾ of the upper handicap limit; i.e. a maximum of a 6-goal player in an 8-goal tournament; a maximum of a 4-goal player in a 5-goal tournament, etc.

Substitutes

If a player or official is sick, injured, or intoxicated to the extent that he endangers the safety of himself, or others, he must be removed from the game. Should a player be removed or request to be removed, a substitution will be allowed, namely at the beginning of the next chukka. Should the situation be more urgent, the umpire can stop the play clock and allow the injured or ineligible player to leave, but the substitute will not be allowed to join until the beginning of the following chukka. While any number of substitutions may be made, all substitutes must be eligible with regard to membership and handicap. If, owing to a substitution, the team handicap changes, the highest aggregate handicap at any point during the game shall be considered the team's handicap for that game.

Should a player be removed from the game and an eligible player is not available, the team will be allowed to continue to play, one member short. And, as per the previous rule, no handicap change will be allowed. Should the play be stopped owing to a player needing immediate substitution, more than one player may be substituted for as long as their team remains qualified.

PLAYERS' APPAREL

All players must wear a helmet with a chinstrap that is fitted properly. Teams' jerseys should be distinguishable enough not to lead to confusion on the field. If two teams' jerseys are similar enough in colour that it makes them difficult to distinguish, the team lower in the tournament draw will be instructed to change.

All of a player's personal equipment should avoid having sharp protrusions that could injure another player. The HPA goes a step further and states: 'Players are expected to be well turned out so that the reputation of the sport is enhanced. This includes presentations and prize-giving.' While not actually stated in the USPA rule book, this is a good suggestion for all.

The USPA rule book does not give an acceptable length for spurs; the HPA notes that spurs must not be longer than 1¼ inches. It also states that whips must not be longer than 48 inches.

MOUNTS

Although equines that are used for the sport of polo are called polo 'ponies', there are no height or breed restrictions for a polo match.

The rules regarding mounts are designed to protect both riders and their mounts from dangerous situations or perceived abuse. Any pony who is deemed dangerous, or does not appear to be under control, shall be removed from the game. No pony may play for more than one team during a tournament. An umpire will ask a player to remove his mount if there is any visible blood on the pony, and they will only be allowed to return after the bleeding has stopped and been cleaned up. If a mount appears unfit, or poorly conditioned for the level of polo at which he is being played, he may be removed from the game. The HPA states that a pony may not play if he has been de-nerved; a process that cuts nerve supply to the foot in an attempt to alleviate pain from a severely damaged foot.

A player should never intentionally strike a mount with any part of the mallet, neither will abuse of spurs or whips be tolerated. Unnecessary or excessive use of the whip is classified as:

- slash whipping – loud and repeated strokes;
- over-whipping – in excess of three strokes or when a mount is labouring;
- heavy whipping – following a missed play.

While both governing bodies, the USPA and the HPA, are concerned with the welfare of the animals involved, the HPA state that a veterinary surgeon registered with the Royal College of Veterinary Surgeons (MRCVS) must attend each tournament, and every club should have a welfare officer appointed.

Another regulation that the HPA states that the USPA doesn't, is the requirement of all ponies to have with them a passport obtained through the HPA, and a vaccination record approved by a veterinarian who is not the animal's owner.

Mount's equipment

To protect polo ponies during a game, no shoes with any kind of projection are allowed, except for a dull heel calk on the hind shoes. Ponies often overreach when performing the athletic movements that polo demands, and any kind of outer rim or toe grab can catch and cut their forelegs.

No equipment is allowed that will interfere with the pony's vision.

The USPA rulebook requires bandages on the forelegs, and encourages the use of bandages on the hind legs, but does not require this.

The HPA rulebook states that ponies (including the umpire's) must wear bandages on all four legs.

The HPA states that all ponies 'are expected to be well turned out', and even has an award given out at the end of a tournament for the best turned-out pony. They go on to provide a list of items of equipment that are prohibited:

- a noseband, headpiece or headcollar that incorporates wire or any sharp material;

- a hackamore or bitless bridle (these may be used in practice chukkas at the discretion of the club);

- blinkers or any form of noseband or other equipment that obstructs the vision of the pony;

- the mouthpiece of any bit, whether single or double, of not less than ¼ inch diameter at its narrowest point;

- the total cheek length of a curb bit may not exceed 6 inches;

- a tongue tie, unless inspected by a MRCVS immediately prior to the chukka. The tongue tie must be removed as soon as the pony leaves the field of play.

DUTIES AND AUTHORITY OF OFFICIALS

Committee

Every official event must have an overseeing committee appointed by the USPA, HPA or the host club. The duties of creating a schedule, performing the draw, coordination of other officials, and organising all of the other necessities for conducting a tournament fall to this committee. Should a question or complaint regarding eligibility or rules come up at any time other than during a game, the committee is the group responsible for resolutions.

Umpires and referee

All tournaments should have at least two mounted umpires and a referee on the side, or three mounted umpires. Any and all rules, violations, incidents or questions (including ones that are not provided for by the

USPA or HPA Rule Books) that arise during the game shall be decided on by the umpires. Before and after the game, the committee decides. In the event that the two mounted umpires do not agree, the line referee will decide on the call, or call offsetting penalties. (This means that a penalty of equal weight is called on each team, in which case nothing happens.) In the event of three mounted umpires not agreeing on a call, no foul shall be called.

Goal judges

Goal judges should be set up at both goals and must keep a vigilant eye on the game. If a ball crosses the end line between the goal-posts, the goal judge raises and waves his flag above his head, signalling a goal. If the ball crosses the end line outside of a goal-post, the goal judge will wave his flag below his waist, and place a ball appropriately for a knock in. The appropriate spot for a knock in should be within a foot of the place where the ball crossed over originally, on even ground, but not closer than 4 yards to the goal-posts or either of the sideboards.

Timekeeper and scorer

The committee shall be in charge of appointing an official timekeeper and scorer for every regulation game. The timekeeper is in charge of keeping track of the time during the chukka and between chukkas, and sounding the horn (or bell) once for the 30-second warning and then twice at the end of the chukka. The scorer is in charge of keeping track of the number of goals, and the fouls committed by each team during the match.

GAME FACILITIES

Playing field

A regulation outdoor polo field is 300 yards in length by 160 yards in width. If boarded on the long sides, the width must be 160 yards. The ends shall remain unboarded to allow the ball to roll out of bounds. If a field does have sideboards, they should be taller than 11 inches Every field should have a marked centre line to make it easier to identify visually where to line up for the throw-in. It is recommended, but not required, that the 30-, 40- and 60-yard lines at the ends of each side of the field be marked for shooting penalty shots.

The goal-posts should be set up at the centre of the end lines, 8 yards apart. They should be at least 10 feet high and fragile enough to break upon a collision.

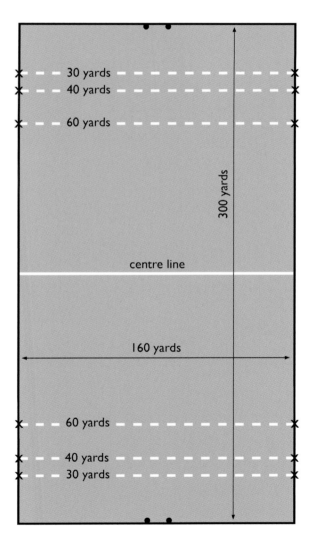

Layout of a polo field.

Equipment for the game and games officials

All of the necessary equipment should be provided to the game officials. An outdoor polo ball must be between 3–3½ inches in diameter, and 3½–4½ ounces in weight. Ponies, whistles, pick-up sticks, ball bags and uniforms must be provided for each umpire. The referee must have an official copy of the appropriate rule book; the timekeeper must have a stopwatch and horn or bell; the scorer must have an official score sheet; the goal judges must be provided with flags and uniforms.

THE GAME

General format

Games will have between four and six chukkas. Four minutes will be allowed between each chukka for players to change mounts, equipment, get a drink, etc. Every game should also have a 10-minute half-time.

Duration of periods

Two minutes before each chukka, the horn must be sounded, calling 'Riders Up'. Two horns shall sounds at the beginning of each chukka. Once begun, each chukka will be 7½ minutes long. Before the end of each chukka, the horn will sound once to give a 30-second warning, and twice when the period clock runs out.

The play clock only stops when the umpire's whistle is blown. The play clock does not stop when a goal is scored or the ball goes out of bounds. During throw-ins, the clock begins the moment the ball leaves the umpire's hand. During knock-ins, the clock begins the moment the ball is hit into play.

Should play stop because of the ball going out of bounds, a goal being scored, or for any other reason besides a foul, after the 30-second warning, the chukka will be deemed finished. If the play stops owing to a foul after the 30-second warning, the penalty will be taken and the chukka will then terminate. Should a penalty be called less than 5 seconds before the end of a chukka, the play clock will be reset to 5 seconds and the penalty taken.

If the end of the game results in a tied score, the committee has two options in respect of a tiebreaker, the choice being made after full time. One option is to play an overtime chukka until one side scores a goal. The other option is a 'shootout'. In the event of a shootout, the players will be allowed 4 minutes after the last regular chukka to change ponies. Once the players are back on the field, the umpires will choose a goal. Each team then takes turns hitting a 40-yard free shot at an undefended goal. After every player on both teams has had a chance to hit, the points will be added up. If the score is still tied, another shootout period will commence until a winner is declared.

Winning of game: goals

Simply, the team with the most goals by the end of the game wins. The combination of goals awarded by handicap, goals scored on the field, and goals awarded from penalties will designate the winning team.

Goals awarded by handicap are counted slightly differently between the USPA and HPA:

For a USPA game, the goals awarded by handicap are determined by finding the difference between the aggregate total of players' handicaps on both teams. This number is then divided by 6, and then multiplied by the number of chukkas to be played in the game.

For a HPA game, the goals awarded by handicap are determined by finding the difference between the aggregate total of player's handicaps on both teams. This number is then multiplied by the number of chukkas to be played and then divided by 6.

Both of these formulae will result in the same numbers, but it's interesting to note the difference. If either formula results in a fraction of a goal, any fraction over ½ a goal will be counted as a full goal.

Commencement, interruption, and resumption of play

How play commences

At the beginning of the game, both teams line up on the centre line in parallel rows. The umpire bowls the ball between the two rows, under-hand and with force. The two teams must stay on their side of the middle line, and not crowd or rush the umpire.

The line up.

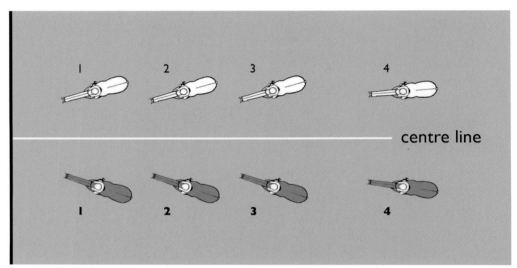

How play is interrupted

The play clock will not stop until the umpire blows his whistle, or the chukka time runs out. The umpire will blow the whistle and stop play when:

- a player hits the ball, or the ball bounces off of his mount and ends up crossing that player's own end line;
- a foul is called;
- the ball breaks or becomes buried;
- a player or mount is injured;
- a player falls off;

- tack or some other equipment breaks, resulting in a dangerous situation;

- a helmet falls off; or

- the umpire decides that play should be suspended owing to darkness or bad weather.

A broken mallet, however, is not considered broken equipment resulting in a dangerous situation. In case your mallet breaks during a match, you should have a couple within reach, or with a groom on the side lines, but play will not be stopped while you switch them over.

How play is resumed

When the ball is knocked out of bounds at the end line, it will be placed on the line within a foot of where it went out. Both teams should be given a reasonable amount of time to get into position, but must be further than 30 yards from the ball. Should play be stopped owing to a broken ball, the teams will line up at the point the umpire blew his whistle and a throw-in will occur. If the ball goes out of bounds across a sideboard, the players will line up for a throw-in, facing the boards where the ball went out, at least 10 yards inside the sideboards. At the end of a chukka, wherever the ball was when the final whistle blew is where the throw-in will take place to begin the next chukka.

Personal fouls

Line of the ball

The 'line of the ball' is an invisible line that projects in front of and behind the ball, in the direction of travel. Even if a ball stops and falls dead during a game, the line of the ball remains in the direction it was travelling before it stopped.

Right of way

Similarly to the line of the ball, throughout the entire game, the player closest to the ball shall have a lane projecting in front of and behind him designated as the right of way. Once this right of way has been established, no other player should enter or cross the right of way except at a safe enough speed and distance not to risk a collision. The right of way changes and follows the line of the ball when the line changes. Should the line of the ball change suddenly, and a player find himself in the right of way, but without the necessary claim to it, he must vacate it as quickly as possible. While vacating the right of way, the player must not make a play for the ball, otherwise he will be committing a foul.

Another way to 'see' the right of way, is that when one player is following the ball, riding to the left of the line (i.e. with the ball positioned on his offside) and another player is coming to meet the ball, the player established on the line has the right of way.

When two players are not established on the line, but riding to meet the ball, the player with the lesser angle at the ball will have the right of way over someone approaching the ball at a greater angle. Also, should the angles be similar, the player who would have the line on his offside will take the right of way over the player who would have the ball on his nearside. When two players are making a play at the ball, riding in the same direction, those two players have the right of the way over a single player. If, at any time, the player established on the line of the ball, with the right of way, has to check or alter speed and/or direction to avoid a collision, a foul has occurred.

Stopping on the ball

A player who is in control of the ball, established on the line, is allowed to slow down and stop on the ball as long as the players following behind have sufficient opportunity to steer around said player. Often you will see a player try to pass the ball to a teammate, only to hit it slightly short. The second teammate will stop on the line of the ball, or slow down to wait for the ball to roll within reach. This is allowed, assuming there isn't another player, established on the line in the right of way, coming up behind him.

Also, you'll often see a strong player take control of the ball and, seeing that no opponents can legally make a play against him, he will check up and stop with the ball, allowing his teammates to get downfield to a better position. This is allowed, but the player with the ball will only be allowed one tap before being required to make a strong forward hit, or run with the ball. The reason for this rule is to keep the play moving without interruption.

Dangerous riding

Polo is inherently dangerous, but we must make every effort to reduce the risk as much as possible, to ourselves and to our fellow players. Using excessive force during a ride-off, or coming in for a ride-off at a severe angle, will be classified as 'dangerous riding'. This is one of those fouls where it is left to the discretion of the umpires as to what is considered 'excessive' and 'severe'. Things that the umpires will take into consideration are:

- the speeds of the two mounts involved – if one mount is moving significantly slower than the other;

- the relative sizes of the two mounts;

- the position of the two mounts in relation to each other – if one mount is dramatically ahead or behind the other;

- the readiness of the receiving mount – if one player is blind-sided by another.

If the mount receiving the ride-off loses balance, or is tripped up by another mount, a dangerous riding foul should be called. Two players on the same team sandwiching an opposing player, or one player pushing an opponent into a swing or right of way of another player so as to make a dangerous situation will also be called as a foul.

Rough or abusive play

This one is a no-brainer. Any player grabbing or striking another player or mount with a hand, head, arm, elbow or mallet will be dismissed from the rest of the game without the opportunity for a substitution.

Improper use of the mallet

Following on the previous rule, using the mallet for anything other than hooking or hitting the ball is a foul. When hooking, you must be on the same side of your opponent as the ball. Reaching underneath the neck of your opponent's pony for the hook, or worse, between the legs, is extremely dangerous. You should only hook when your opponent is in the act of hitting the ball, and only when your opponent's mallet is below shoulder height. Any 'high hooks' will be called as a foul. You are allowed to 'strike' your opponent's mallet with your own, but only below shoulder height and with reasonable force.

Once the whistle has been called, the ball is 'dead', and no one is allowed to hit the ball intentionally. This rule really applies to the player who hits the ball after the whistle has blown in frustration or anger.

Appealing for a foul

As previously stated, the only person on a team qualified to discuss a foul with an umpire is the team captain, and only for the purposes of clarification. No other player may appeal to the umpire in any way for a foul.

Carrying the ball

No player may intentionally catch, kick, or carry the ball. A player may block the ball with any part of his body, but if the ball gets lodged in a player's tack or person, the whistle must be blown and the play begun again from that spot.

Interference with play

No outside person is allowed on the playing field during a match. A dismounted player is not allowed to interfere with the game at all. If a player needs to change his pony or mallet, he must ride to the sideboards, or beyond the end lines to change so that any assistant is not in danger of affecting the game at all.

Unsportsmanlike conduct

Any action that may be construed as unsportsmanlike conduct will not be allowed. This includes actions such as:

- yelling or verbal abuse;
- disrespectful behaviour towards anyone;
- delaying the game falsely;
- raising the mallet or swinging the mallet in an appeal for a foul.

Repeated fouls

If a player continually commits the same foul, either carelessly or deliberately, the umpire is encouraged to exact increasingly more severe penalties each time.

Penalties

Selection of penalties

When deciding which penalty should accompany a foul, the umpire must take into consideration:

- severity of the foul committed;
- location of the foul on the field;
- position of the players with regard to the foul;
- frequency that this same foul has occurred.

Definition of penalties

Penalties are defined by number, as follows.

Penalty No. 1

Usually reserved for severe fouls, a Penalty No. 1 will give the fouled team one goal, the ends will not change, and the play will resume by a throw-in on the 10-yard line closest to the fouling team's goal.

Penalty No. 2

A free shot on goal from the 30-yard line against the fouling team's goal, or, at the discretion of the fouled team's captain, at the place where the foul occurred. When lined up for the shot, the other members of the fouled team must be behind the ball, and the fouling team may not make any attempt to block the ball. The fouled team gets one shot at goal. If they do not score, the fouling team is allowed a knock-in from where the ball came to rest.

Penalty No. 3

Penalty No. 3 has the same standards as No. 2, except that the ball is placed at the 40-yard line, and may be defended or not.

In 20+ goal games, the umpire may decide that the Penalty No. 3 will be defended. If defending, the fouling team must position themselves behind their end line and must not come onto the field until the ball is hit (or hit at). The fouled team will get one shot at the ball. If it does not result in a goal, the defending team has the right to the ball, and play will begin from that spot.

Penalty No. 4

A Penalty No. 4 is a free shot from the 60-yard line. Both teams are allowed to position themselves anywhere on, or off, the field, so long as it is more than 30 yards away from the ball.

Penalty No. 5

At the umpire's discretion, a Penalty No. 5 can be a free hit from the middle of the field, or from the point of the infraction. Both teams are allowed to position themselves as they see fit, so long as they're 30 yards away from the ball.

Penalty No. 6

A Penalty No. 6 occurs when a player hits the ball over his own end line, resulting in the fouled team receiving a free hit from the 60-yard line opposite where the ball crossed the line.

Penalty No. 7

In the event that a player is injured to the point where retirement from the game is necessary, as a result of a foul, the captain of the fouled team may order the removal of a player from the opposite team. The fouling team's player who is dismissed will be the one whose handicap is equal to, or the nearest above, the injured player.

Penalty No. 8

A Penalty No. 8 is simply the dismissal of a mount from the playing field. This could be the result of the mount being injured, or unruly, or wearing unallowable equipment. Should it be caused by the latter, once the equipment is removed, the mount may be allowed to play again.

Penalty No. 9

A Penalty No. 9 is the forfeit of the game.

Penalty No. 10

The umpire may dismiss a player for all, or a portion, of the game. The umpire may, or may not, allow a replacement of the player, depending on the severity of the foul committed.

Conclusion

IN THIS BOOK I'VE GONE over the history of polo, the pony's equipment, the player's equipment, horsemanship, the biomechanics of the different swings, game play and strategy, and a breakdown of the USPA and HPA rulebooks. I know no book can replace the time spent in the saddle, actually riding, hitting the ball, or playing, but a well-rounded polo player must study the sport and assimilate information from multiple resources. Your trainers and fellow polo players are a treasure-trove of guidance and information. Much can also be learned from watching instructional videos and videos of games, and from investigating other equestrian disciplines and listening to seasoned horsemen's stories.

My sincere hope is that you have learned something new from this book that will fill in the gaps in your polo education. Educated players make better players, which makes for better polo.

Here's to better polo!

Polo Exercises

The following exercises will help develop your riding and playing skills.

Riding without stirrups

As often as possible and for as long as possible, ride without the stirrups. Cross the stirrup leathers and irons over the pony's withers to prevent the irons banging against the pony's elbows. Any rider of any discipline will tell you that this is the very best way to get more established seat in the saddle, to develop your balance and the muscles needed to become a great rider.

Lungeing exercises

If you have someone who will lunge you, you can do these exercises at a walk, trot and canter without much worry. If not, practise them at a walk on your own on a safe, stable mount.

1. While riding, reach your right hand down your right leg and hold the top of the stirrup iron. Make sure to keep your lower leg position hanging loosely by the girth; make sure your foot does not slide backwards. Repeat on the left.

2. While keeping your lower legs in position, slide your right hand down your left leg until you can reach the top of your stirrup iron or as far

down as you can without injuring yourself. Ride for a time in this position, stretching your hamstrings, back and shoulders. Repeat with your left hand.

3. Seated deep in the saddle, turn to the right and run your right hand along the top of your mount's haunches. Repeat on the other side.

Wooden horse

If your club has an enclosed wooden horse, take advantage of it. You cannot spend enough time practising your swing. Even if your club does not have this equipment, find an elevated surface such as a fence, and practise your swing, with or without a ball.

At first, begin by spending equal amounts of time on all four swings (offside fore, offside back, nearside fore, nearside back). While a good majority of your swings on the playing field will be offside fore shots, you need to have a good foundation in all of them. Once your offside fore is well established, warm that swing up, dial in your hand to eye coordination, but spend most of your time focusing on the less common swings.

In addition to these four basic shots, begin hitting open and tail back shots from the offside and nearside. Begin practising your offside and nearside neck shots. Although less common, these shots can be powerful weapons in your armoury and it may be worthwhile having a professional demonstrate them and give you some coaching in how and when to play them. It takes 10,000 correct repetitions before a swing becomes muscle memory, and there's no need to wear a pony out while you practise. Most clubs, also, will not charge you for time on the wooden horse, so it's an economical way to practise your swing.

Tag

Playing tag with a friend will not only help you anticipate your opponents' moves, it will also help polish your pony's reflexes. If you've ever been caught out of position and left behind as an opponent runs away with the ball, you will understand how frustrating it can be. You stretch as far out of the saddle as possible, reaching for any possible hook that could foil your opponent's next swing, but you're always out of reach. Playing tag will help you prevent these instances from occurring. It's played exactly how it sounds: without a mallet, chase your friend around the field, trying to touch his or her back. Once you tag them, it's your turn to be tagged. The evasive manoeuvres you'll find yourself doing also mimic real game play for your pony, helping fine-tune their responses and make them handier.

Stick and ball

Once you feel comfortable and confident with your swing on the wooden horse, stick and balling is the next step in your polo development. This will help you hone in your hand to eye coordination, and help you develop your timing, both in respect of meeting the ball accurately and executing the shot. Stick and balling is when you hit the ball around an open field. Begin first at a walk, concentrating on your body position, your mallet position and your timing. You can begin with half swings, to get your arm used to the pendulum-like motion of the swing. Try to swing the mallet as slowly as possible. Once you're comfortable at walk, graduate to trot and then to canter. Also be conscious of your pony's fitness level, and never sacrifice your pony for your practice.

Dribbling

Handy stick-work can make or break a player. Learn to dribble the ball in short, quick taps. Begin by approaching the ball, and tapping it in a circle to your right. Begin again at walk, then trot, then canter. Remember, however, that in a game, the more taps you take to get around the circle and turn the ball, the more opportunity there is for you to miss it, or your opponent to intercept it. Try to turn the ball through a half-circle in two or three taps. Always keep the ball in front of your pony's shoulder as you're dribbling. Keep the motions of the mallet restricted to the wrist, as these are not full motions that require the shoulder and the elbow.

Once you're experienced in dribbling the ball around to the right, practise in a circle to the left on the nearside. This is much trickier, but worth the effort.

Backing drill

In a circle to the right, beginning at walk and gradually increasing to canter, back the ball out and away from your pony. This should put it back on the line of your circle for you to pick it up and back it to yourself again.

Shooting at goal

Begin by setting up a series of balls at the penalty shot lines, i.e. the 10-, 30-, 40- and 60-yard lines. Games can be won or lost on penalty shots, and it is easy to succumb to pressure when the game is on the line, and you have two teams, umpires and fans watching you. Practise these shots *ad nauseam* until they become second nature to you. That way, when the pressure is on, you'll be able to shoot confidently.

Set up a series of balls at varying distances from the goal and varying angles and, while travelling in circles, practise approaching the ball and hitting it through the goal-mouth at different angles.

Hitting to a spot

Go out to the field with two balls. Hit one ball about 10 yards up, hit the second ball 10 yards past that one and leapfrog them around the field. This will get you into the practice of always hitting the ball to a spot, not just an indeterminate place down the field.

INDEX